KEEP
AN EYE
ON THAT
MUMMY

KEEP
AN EYE
ON THAT
MUMMY

By Nancy Kriplen

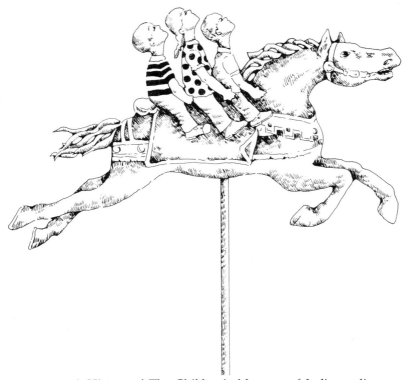

A History of The Children's Museum of Indianapolis

Standard Book Number 0-9608982-0-4

For information, contact
The Children's Museum
P.O. Box 3000
Indianapolis, Indiana 46206

Printed in the United States of America

Edited by Margaret M. Maxwell
Designed by Sheila M. Jackson
Indexed by Paula Corpuz, Amy Schutt

To honor twenty-one years of achievement
with the Children's Museum,
this book has been published
as a tribute
to Mildred S. Compton.

"I very much enjoyed the visit to the Museum. I liked the mummy the best. Will you do me a favor? Keep an eye on that mummy and let me know if anything strange happens."

From a child's letter to the Children's Museum

CONTENTS

PREFACE

Just as it has been the caretaker of the history of others, the Children's Museum certainly should collect and document its own past, said the museum's representative. It was our first discussion about the book the Children's Museum wished to publish which would chronicle the events and people who had turned an idea into a thriving institution.

For any business or organization to don the mantle of publisher for a work about itself which the writer insists must be clear-eyed and complete is not always easy. Yet this the museum staff did with grace. I was given complete cooperation and total access to all material sought; nothing in the manuscript was censored. As an evaluation specialist commented a few years ago in a report on the Children's Museum, "Only a strong group of people and strong institution could see the positive and constructive benefits of a self-study."

Thanks, first of all, must go to two people in particular: the museum's director, Mildred Compton, who patiently sat still for hour upon hour of interviews; and Margaret Maxwell, the museum's talented publications editor who, with great skill and perception, as well as good humor, edited the manuscript.

Special tribute also should be paid to two people who generously shared with me their time and remarkable memories of the museum's early days, but did not live to see the publication of this book. Estelle Preston Bell died December 2, 1981; Hillis Howie died June 2, 1982. Because of Howie's earlier detective work, I was able to make contact with Stewart

Springer, the museum's first curator, who was also most helpful.

Assistance and information came from many connected with the museum—past and present members of the staff, board of trustees and Children's Museum Guild, as well as other participants in, or observers of, the affairs of the museum through the years: Reily Adams, Alan Appel, Jack Appel, Jane Baxter, Harry Bell, Lisa Berezin, Tom Billings, Alex Black, Rosemary Skaggs Carr, Jim Casey, David Cassady, Leslie Clumb, Dwight Crandell, Katie DeGroff, Allen Denmark, Lee Dorste, Berkley Duck Jr., Jack Ebbeler, Mary Jane Teeters Eichacker, Otto Frenzel, Bob Gillman, Nanci Golden-McCollum, Shelly Gorny, Eric Gyllenhaal, John Harris, Kenneth Hartman, Georgia Hendrickson, George Hing, Sheila Jackson, Margaret Jameson, Bob Johnson, Ernie Jones, Polly Jontz, Martha Karatz, Max Knaus, Dessie Partenheimer Koch, Robert LaRue, Mary Latham, Robin Lipp, Liz Main, Malcolm McVie, Bill Norton, Henry Peirce, Jack Rauch, Harley Rhodehamel, Paul Richard, Richard Ruddell, Judi Ryan, LaNita Sanders, Betty Schaab, Carol Slotkin, Suzann Smart, Katharine Smith, Susie Sogard, Steve Sullivan, Jane Sweet, Isabelle Troyer, George Varnes, Kurt Vonnegut, Jr., Myron Vourax, Barbara Werbe, Jeff Windholz, Billie Lou Wood.

I also wish to thank Lloyd Hezekiah, George Kelly, Terry McCarthy and Nancy Paine, all of the Brooklyn Children's Museum; Elaine Gurian, Boston Children's Museum; John Larson, Oriental Institute, University of Chicago; Bradway Wallace, Art Institute of Chicago; Charlotte Holton, American Museum of Natural History; Isabel Martin and Monica Schoultz, Indianapolis Museum of Art; Carl Weinhardt, Jr., Villa Vizcaya Museum and Gardens, Miami, Florida; Professor John Pelton, Butler University; Professor Robert Lindsley, Colgate University; Jim Hurrell, Indiana Central University; Jeanette Matthew and John Straw, Indiana University-Purdue University, Indianapolis; Karl Kalp (former superintendent), Maggie Jackson and Jo Wolf, Indianapolis Public Schools; Gordon Thompson and Marie Rice (former teacher), Orchard School; Nancy Kampovsky, Indianapolis Department of Parks and Recreation.

Exceptional help came from Kathy Bugman, Debby Flynn, Patty Matkovic and Linda Walton of the Indiana Division, Indiana State Library. My thanks also to Caroline Dunn (former librarian), Leigh Darbee, Eric Pomroy and Tim Peterson, Indiana Historical Society Library; Randy Ayers, Jean Bowles and Georgia Cravey and children's division and information center personnel of the Indianapolis-Marion County Public Library; and Sandra Fitzgerald and Charlesetta Means, Indianapolis Star-News library. Author William H. A. Carr provided both counsel and encouragement, as did my husband, David Kriplen, who gave the manuscript a wise first reading.

Because this book is intended primarily for general readers, no footnotes have been included. However, a manuscript with footnotes is on file in the archives of the Children's Museum for those who need more information about source material for specific passages.

The day on which I turned in the final chapters of this book I saw, just outside the museum's front door, a tiny, pigtailed 2-year-old. She was holding on tightly to a paper dinosuar bone from a preschool craft class, and sobbing as if her heart would break. Explained her mother, "She doesn't want to leave."

I knew just how she felt.

CHAPTER ONE
A Museum Awakens

The big cat lies quietly, its smooth, black sides shiny in the half-mist, half-rain of early morning. It hunkers down quite alone in a small fringe of two-day-old snow. No giggling, excited children slide down its nose or stretch out in delicious luxury along its broad granite-like back.

They'll not be here for hours yet, the small visitors in boots and sneakers, school buses and strollers, who, from 10 a.m. on, will be trooping in to visit the world's largest children's museum. More than one million of them (and parents, and school teachers, and just plain curious adults), a record number, came during the twelve months preceding. At a dollar each, that would have been more than $1 million. As a matter of fact, however, they paid nothing. The museum is free.

Though the winter solstice is thirty-two days past, on this overcast morning it is still dark in Indianapolis at 7:20 a.m. At the main level reception desk, the night guard, a college student, flicks on the core lights. The five floors of corridors surrounding the building's large, square, central atrium are suddenly, softly illuminated. Not until just before the museum is ready to open are the lights to be turned on over the central core's spiral ramps, up which visitors will stream like moving tinsel on a Christmas tree.

Allen Denmark, foam cup of coffee in hand, unlocks a third-floor storage room and rolls out a large supply cart. He is a big man with a mustache, dressed in the trim, dark brown uniform of the museum's building services department. The cart is loaded with a ladder, broom, vinyl glue, boxes of at least twenty different kinds of light bulbs and several different styles of long-handled tools for reaching burned-out bulbs. There's even a special device for unscrewing broken bulbs, with a shield to catch falling fragments.

For 2½ hours every morning, Denmark follows the same top-to-bottom pattern in waking up the 203,000-square-foot museum—fifth floor galleries first. He flips switches in an electrical closet next to the Science Spectrum gallery; the gallery is immediately bright with light. Suspended from the ceiling are giant, colorful banners appliqued with the faces and names of famous scientists. Archimedes and Louis Pasteur billow gently in the breeze from an air inlet in the ceiling above. From somewhere in the rear of the gallery comes the faint sound of computer music.

Looking up constantly for dark, lifeless bulbs, Denmark pushes the cart clockwise around the atrium. He spots a cobweb in the corner of one of the recessed concrete squares with which the ceilings of this stark, clean-lined, contemporary building are honeycombed. Out comes the long-handled broom; the cobweb is no more.

He moves down a side hall, turns lights on in restrooms, makes a mental note that a fire extinguisher is missing from its accustomed spot. From another separate electrical control room the lights are turned on in the large galleries of the fifth floor's southwest corner. The plain, bare bulbs around the mirrored canopy of the museum's carousel come on suddenly in an appropriately circus-like blaze of garish light. The spar-varnished backs of three giraffes, three stags, three goats, a lion, a tiger and assorted horses gleam.

Forty-one hand-carved animals (twenty-four stationary, seventeen "jumpers") and one sandbag wait expectantly in a circle. The eighteenth jumper, a black horse with a cluster of purple grapes decorating its bridle, is on a month's R and R in the museum's conservation studio downstairs. All the jumpers need their paint and varnish touched up frequently, for this room-filling structure is, in fact, a real, working carousel. It operated for thirty-nine years in a park five miles north of this spot. Normally, the brassy, cheerful music from its Wurlitzer band organ drifts down through the central atrium to greet visitors as they walk in the front door. But since today is a school day, the music and the operating mechanism of the carousel won't be turned on until 2 p.m.

The morning's first bulb change (a sixty-watt Crown-Glo, a bulb which spreads light out evenly from a short distance and allows people to walk up and look closely at things without standing in their own shadow) comes in the Toy Train Treasures gallery. It's a stepladder job because the bulb is in a metal shade.

Even without walking through the entire maze of nine-foot-tall cases, Denmark is able to spot dead bulbs by checking the reflections in the glass. In the cases, some five thousand pieces—engines, cars and accessories—are displayed. It's the largest public display of toy trains in this country and probably the world. In the middle of the gallery, at a small participatory display ("Can you match each train to its correct manufacturer?"), Denmark punches the Lionel, Ives and American Flyer answer buttons to see that none has burned out.

The lights also have been turned on in the nearby, but separate, operating train layout, and a tiny toy derrick swings eerily in an invisible draft of circulating air. Not until the museum opens at 10 a.m. will the exhibit's staff operator start the five O-gauge and two HO-gauge trains rushing through the layout's 1,156 square feet of track and Lilliputian villages.

Continuing around the core to the northwest corner, Denmark selects one of the keys from the jangling ring of twenty-nine chained to his belt, unlocks a panel under the large Ball doll house and switches on the lights. If one of the tiny rooms is dark (as is the attached carriage house), the bulb change will be made later by the exhibits preparator.

With Denmark holding securely on to a bar in the back, the supply cart rolls easily—almost too easily—down the ramps to the floor below. (In a pamphlet for visitors, the museum recommends that people in wheelchairs use the elevators.) The rust-colored, tweed carpet covering the ramps and corridors is spotless. A private, industrial cleaning firm comes in at night, its mandate to clean up to the edges of the exhibits; the museum staff takes it from there.

The museum's own staff housekeeper, with cleaning rags, window spray and green feather duster in hand, is also making her morning rounds. She'll whisk the dust from some of the sturdy, large pieces, such as the 1940 Maserati race car and Lil Chip, the perky, little, red aerobatic biplane which sits, bathed in light (bulbs all O.K.), patiently waiting for a chance to do another Immelmann. Other, more fragile, exhibits, such as the early cars on display in the back of the Americana gallery, will be dusted by the exhibits preparator.

Denmark checks the rest of the Americana gallery, including the "fires" (orange light bulbs behind moving silver and orange metallic strips) burning in the fireplace of the full-size log cabin and under the black iron pot right outside the cabin door. The pot actually is a special, modern one; it's used to melt wax for Saturday morning candle-making demonstrations. The cabin, though, is what it seems to be: the actual, one-time home of Indiana pioneers.

Across the building in Playscape ("Play is a child's work" proclaims a purple banner), Denmark walks the length of the bright, apple-green room quickly making sure that all is as it should be in this area of climbing, drawing, pretending activities for children ages 2 to 7. On the wall near the Water Works, ten yellow plastic smocks and one red-and-white-checked one hang from round pegs. Another building services staff member has already completed his daily task of draining, scrubbing and refilling the shallow pools in this water play area. By the end of every day, sand from the nearby Sand Dome has somehow gotten into the Water Works. (Any parent who has tried to keep a backyard wading pool clean would understand.)

From somewhere in the building comes the loud whine of a hammerdrill making room in the concrete walls for the conduits and wires of the museum's new Wang 2200 VS 80 minicomputer system. Over the next fifty-six months, the computer is scheduled to take on not only the museum's financial affairs, but also such things as school tour scheduling and collections record-keeping.

On the north side of the third floor, Denmark pushes his cart into an area closed to the public. In this private world of the exhibits design department, he checks lights in the photography darkroom, storage areas and workrooms. In one of the offices, Superman, muscles bulging, blue arm thrust up, leans against the wall, ready to take his place in an upcoming temporary exhibit about comic strip art. In the office next door, a meticulous scale model (½ inch equals 1 foot) of a new, semi-permanent gallery of miniature rooms sits on top of a three-legged work stand. Nearby, in a large workroom, a designer studies fanned-out swatches of dyed cloth, trying to decide which colors would best set off the bird eggs in a nature study drawer ("Can you guess which birds and eggs go together?").

The second burned-out bulb of the morning (a seventy-five-watt, ellipsoidal reflector flood) turns up by a ten-foot-tall stuffed polar bear in front of the Eskimo exhibit. Denmark changes the bulb, then walks on through the exhibit, pushing a large, red button which turns on an audio-visual show. "The daily life of the Eskimos was governed by the harmony of the seasons . . . ," a cheerful recorded voice explains to no one.

As Denmark throws more switches, the empty galleries suddenly fill with the sounds of Yoruba drums and Bambara xylophones coming from a thatched hut in the Africa gallery around the corner. During the recorded "Rhythm in Life" program, various instruments in a case at the back of the hut are lighted as examples of their sounds are played and explained. The program will automatically turn off after ten minutes. All will remain quiet until a curious visitor places his hand on the metal hand print covering the touch-activated mechanism. Denmark retrieves two cardboard light bulb packages from the base of the towering model of a Fulani dancer on stilts, and the cart, sounding not unlike an exotic African instrument, rumbles off down the corridor.

In the opposite corner of the building, in a small alcove with wall and ceiling tomb paintings copied from a thirteenth century B.C. Egyptian tomb lies the mummy Wenuhotep. Her sleep has been undisturbed by any light bulb changes since the new museum building opened in 1976.

Denmark also checks the bulb situation in a recessed, almost hidden, glass-topped "grave" across the aisle. In it is a curled-up, ancient body, preserved for the past five thousand years because of its original burial in hot, dry Egyptian desert sand. In 1898, explains a label, the body was bought by a traveler. It probably had been buried facing west so it could join the setting sun on its journey into the afterworld. Presumably that journey is completed, for in Indianapolis, the body lies facing east and the morning rush hour traffic on Meridian Street.

Around the corner, Denmark discovers that a bulb (fifty-watt reflector flood) illuminating the museum's reassembled mastodon skeleton needs to be replaced. The skeleton was found in 1976 in a bog on the Christensen farm in nearby Greenfield, Indiana. After all possible bones were recovered and studied, only about 30 percent of the animal had to be re-created from plaster resin. For nine months, the reassembly itself was a museum display, with visitors watching through two glass windows as scientists wired bones.

In the northwest corner of the third level, the Decision Shop, a computer game exhibit developed to teach basic economic principles to 10- to 15-year-olds, sits with blank, black screen. In about an hour, when someone from the security staff turns it on, the screen will bloom in a kaleidoscope of color. Anyone approaching it will activate it by breaking a small beam of light near the floor. "HELLO" it will immediately spell out in big orange, green, blue and pink letters. "I'm glad you decided to come over. My name is Focus. I run this shop," it will continue with the enthusiasm of a carnival barker. From the time the museum opens, there will seldom be a time when someone is not seated on the stool, hunched over the keyboard, deciding how much spaceship fuel can safely be traded for food (Star Trader game) or how much of an amusement park's profits should be used for advertising (Carnival game).

Downstairs on the main floor (actually level two), Denmark parks his cart outside the entrance to the simulated limestone cave and walks through the automatic sliding door. He follows the winding, 120-foot-long passage past the small, splashing waterfall, the reproduction stalagmites and stalactites and (a bit like the corned beef sandwich sneaked aboard the Gemini 3 space flight) the fifty-cent piece pressed into wet concrete by an unknown construction worker or museum staffer. All is well with the cave's recessed lights which provide just the right amount of light to keep visitors from tripping, but not so much that the cave illusion is spoiled.

The exit from the cave is near the room in the natural science area where the museum's small collection of live animals is kept. Two American guinea pigs and a buttonquail are having breakfast in their cages. Later in the day, one of the department's staff members will give some of the museum's snakes their once-a-week feeding (and not of live prey either, contrary to popular belief).

Right now this staff member is adding water to the small, outdoor pool (currently plagued by a slow leak) in the walled Nature's Garden area. (Even though there will be no visitors in this outside area until spring, its animal residents need some tending.) She will chop holes in the ice so that the occupants—bluegills, turtles, crustaceans—will have enough oxygen to survive the winter.

Turtles are living in a special pool indoors as well, and Denmark, seeing, without much enthusiasm, that one of this display's bulbs is dead, gingerly lifts a large snapping turtle out of the way so that one of his special tools can be pushed inside to unscrew the bulb.

After a pass through the education wing, where visitors arriving later on school buses will come in through their own special entrance, the cart is trundled on down to the first level and parked in front of the replica Victorian train depot. Denmark walks along the platform past the Reuben Wells, a powerful, wood-burning locomotive which once shepherded cars up and down a steep grade outside Madison, Indiana. He enters the service car on the siding behind the engine and walks through it, sliding open doors and windows which were shut by young visitors the day before. "If it moves, they like to move it," he says patiently.

There are no problems with the sixty-watt bulb in the old-fashioned street light outside the 1890s firehouse or with the "moon" (a large globe light) suspended high above. Next, the cart is taken, via the freight elevator, down into the sub-basement and the bottom level of collections storage, that museum-within-the-museum where the 75,000 items not on display are kept. Denmark parks his cart in a small outer room where there are items to be deaccessioned, that complicated process by which museums now officially get rid of material they don't need and can no longer afford to store. "Inferior quality" is checked on a white, printed deaccession form under a small Scottish doll.

Denmark walks through the next rooms, which are filled both with exotica from foreign lands (sedan chair, armor, tribal masks) and the artifacts of daily American life in more recent times (games, old wicker doll buggies). Lying flat on the floor under a high-legged, white gas range (circa 1930) is a heavy tablet, its upper right corner cracked off. On the tablet is a sea horse wearing a crown, swimming erect between the initials CM.

It is, of course, the old logo of the Children's Museum, an emblem chosen back at the time of the institution's beginnings, long before anyone ever called such things "logos." It is appropriate, somehow, that among the items of other years and other cultures, the museum is preserving this tangible, if imperfect, piece of its own past.

CHAPTER TWO
Brooklyn and Beginnings

Even in 1924, the big old house in Brower Park was still called the Spanish Adams house by some Brooklyn old-timers, though it hadn't been used as a private residence for more than thirty years. The "Adams" was for the family that built the house around 1867. "Spanish" was for the Venezuelan-born Mrs. Adams, an invalid who spoke only Spanish and who was considered, by those neighbors who liked to talk of such things, to be somewhat mysterious.

On top of the tall, Victorian structure was an elaborate cupola; beneath that, a steep-pitched mansard roof twisted and turned in a series of abrupt angles. The tree-studded grounds surrounding the old brick mansion were immaculate, though by October not much color remained in the flower beds. Edging the property was a waist-high, wrought-iron fence with a gate where the curving front walk met the sidewalk along Brooklyn Avenue.

A giant wisteria vine over the porch rustled softly as the visitor walked up the curving path to the front entrance on the first Friday in October, 1924. She was pleasant-faced, of medium height and, at 65, what admirers called stylishly stout. "Mrs. John N. Carey, Indianapolis," she wrote in large, firm letters in the middle of the page in the dark leather guest book. She had come to see for herself a fascinating institution which had been housed in the Adams house for the past twenty-five years, a museum just for children.

The Brooklyn Children's Museum, as the first children's museum in the world, was used to curious adult visitors from other places—places often much more exotic than Indiana. The visitor signing in ahead of Mrs. Carey represented the South Manchuria Railway Company. The one following her came from Lima, Peru.

The museum was about to celebrate its twenty-fifth anniversary, for it had first opened on December 16, 1899. In the 1890s the city-owned Adams house had been leased by the Brooklyn Institute of Arts and Sciences as storage space for books and collections. When these were moved elsewhere, the Victorian mansion and its handsome grounds suddenly became available for a new purpose. And that new purpose, decided the institute, would be a museum especially for children. The nucleus of its two rooms of exhibits were seven hundred natural history specimens purchased from the Musée Scolaire of Emile Deyrolle in Paris.

By 1902, Brooklyn curator-in-chief Anna Billings Gallup had crystallized a philosophy that showed how this new kind of museum was different. "The child must feel," she said, "that the whole plant is for him, that the best is offered to him because of faith in his power to use it, that he has access to all departments, and that he is always a welcome visitor, never an intruder."

By the time of Mrs. Carey's visit in 1924 the two rooms had expanded into two floors of exhibits. There was much for her to see. Cases lined the halls. Cases lined the walls of the rooms, such as the reptile room and the bird room. In the botany room, its radiator topped with pots of plants, a model in one white wall case showed how seeds sprout, and in the insect room there was a beehive.

The museum was particularly proud of its large, light-filled reference library, where children could pick from nine thousand books and read at tables or in arched window seats. More than 60,000 visitors would visit the library before the end of 1924, while the number of visitors to the museum as a whole would reach an amazing 162,000. A variety of programs during the year also attracted many visitors, such as the sixth graders who, on the day of Mrs. Carey's visit, would hurry into the museum after school to see the movie "It's All in the Shreds."

Mrs. Carey had raised four daughters and was now the interested and doting grandmother of seven. But Mary Stewart Carey was more than a fond parent and grandparent. The granddaughter of pioneer Methodist minister Joseph Tarkington (and therefore a cousin of author Booth Tarkington), she was one of the civic and social leaders who made things happen in the Hoosier capital. If New York City-area children had a free museum just for them, she wondered, why shouldn't the children of Indianapolis?

Mrs. Carey's ability to get things done was sometimes facilitated (in the general, gauzy way affluence has of facilitating much in life) by the family money, much of it from the glass business (Stewart-Carey) begun by her father and now presided over by her husband. She was gracious and charming, and smiles notwithstanding, she usually accomplished what she set out to accomplish. Family and friends chuckled at the name "Haverway" she gave the farm she had bought— over her husband's objections—way north of town on Eighty-sixth Street near Spring Mill Road. And a musical skit produced by the Carey daughters at a housewarming party for the new residence included a song sung to the tune of "Put on Your Old Gray Bonnet," which concluded with the words, ". . . and we're glad she had-her-way."

When important things happened in Indianapolis, the Careys were often on hand. In 1907, when President Theodore Roosevelt paid a visit to the home city of his vice president, Charles Warren Fairbanks, Mrs. Carey assisted Mrs. Fairbanks with the elaborate dinner party honoring Roosevelt, given at the vice president's home. Shortly before the evening's festivities were to begin, a crisis developed: there were no cocktails on hand for the president. As the next day's *Indianapolis News* reported, Mrs. Carey quickly called the Columbia Club and ordered forty Manhattans. The mayor volunteered his car for the emergency, and the cocktails were immediately delivered.

In the Brooklyn museum guest book Mrs. Carey had identified herself as president of the Propylaeum (an Indianapolis women's cultural club) and director of the John Herron Art Association. As author John Gunther was to point out a half-century later, Indianapolis was one of the most "organized" cities in the world, and Mrs. Carey was a great joiner. She was an enthusiastic member of the DAR, music clubs, nature clubs, dramatic clubs, and a board member of missions and settlement houses. Two years earlier, in 1922, when her daughter Mary June (Mrs. Fred Appel) was trying to establish a new, progressive private school in Indianapolis, Mrs. Carey let the school use some north-side property she had bought as an investment. The house in the apple orchard at Fiftieth and Meridian gave the new educational institution not only a home but a name, the Orchard School.

Indeed, it was to this Orchard School nucleus, members of the Indianapolis Progressive Education Association, that Mrs. Carey brought back from Brooklyn her first-hand observations of a children's museum. (In addition to Brooklyn, there were already well-known children's museums in Boston, started in 1913, and Detroit, started in 1917.) For the past year, a group within the progressive association had been struggling to develop a way (no one was yet sure of the structure) to circulate to school classrooms the natural history and Indian specimens stored in the Indiana State House. "The marvelous collection of museum material now buried in the State House," Faye Henley, the new director of Orchard School, had called it in informal remarks at a reception in her honor in November 1923.

The state museum's curator, William H. Hershman, himself a retired school superintendent and college president, had responded with enthusiasm to the idea. He suggested that the traveling musem committee get details from the Field Museum in Chicago and a museum in Milwaukee which had similar projects. However, he warned, "To make this work . . . will require a large amount of money . . . and this money the State of Indiana will not pay as long as we are groaning under the present exorbitant taxation." Mindful of the Chicago benefactor who had donated $250,000 to the Field Museum operation, he added, "If you know of one or more public-spirited men who have the means at hand, it might be possible to get him, or them, interested in a public donation."

The public-spirited man with a quarter of a million dollars apparently did not rush forward, and Hershman, sidelined by a serious accident, was unable to do more than offer advice. The committee then consulted Rousseau McClellan, a respected natural science teacher at Shortridge High School, who suggested that, instead of traveling exhibits, the museum have a fixed base. Actually, she recommended many fixed bases: a museum in each of the city parks. Nothing developed from this idea, but at least the interest was there.

Upon her return to Indianapolis, Mrs. Carey also discussed what she had seen in Brooklyn with two friends, Eliza Browning, a fellow DAR officer and former director of the Indianapolis Public Library; and Florence Fitch, the Pratt Institute-trained director of art instruction for the Indianapolis Public Schools. After getting their counsel, she presented the idea for a children's museum in Indianapolis to Woman's Rotary (of which she was, naturally, a member) and asked this organization to lend its support.

On November 10, 1924, the three women met at Miss Fitch's, this time joined by Murray Dalman, director of the reference and research department of the Indianapolis Public Schools, to discuss the advisability of establishing a children's museum. Who else, they pondered, should be asked to join their nucleus, and if any articles were to be donated to such a museum, where could they be stored?

After a conference between Mrs. Carey and Faye Henley, it was decided that the Progressive Education Association would host a general public meeting in early December. Things were moving quickly—only two months had elapsed since Mrs. Carey's visit to Brooklyn. Penny postcards, mailed out in late November, announced, "The Progressive Education Association of Indianapolis invites all who are interested in the foundation of a Children's Museum to attend a meeting to be held Tuesday evening, December the second, at eight o'clock in the Cropsey Auditorium, Central Library."

Indianapolis did not exactly rush to answer the call. A disappointing nineteen Indianapolis citizens, in addition to Dalman and the four women, appeared in the downtown auditorium that evening. Among the nineteen were Mary June

Appel; J. Arthur MacLean, director of the John Herron Art Institute; Dr. Christopher B. Coleman, director of the Indiana Historical Bureau; plus representatives from Woman's Rotary, the Parent-Teacher Association and the *Indianapolis News.*

With Miss Fitch presiding, speakers discussed other museums in the state, the Brooklyn Children's Museum, the state museum's need for larger quarters and the usefulness of museum material to school children. An organizational committee was formed with Mrs. Carey as chairman, Miss Henley as secretary pro tem and eight other members: Miss Browning, Miss Fitch, Dalman, MacLean, Coleman, Charles Rush, director of the Indianapolis Public Library; Mrs. Charles H. Smith, president of the Parent-Teacher Association of Indianapolis; and Mrs. David Ross, president of the Indianapolis Free Kindergarten Association.

In a rush of enthusiasm, the new committee scheduled a meeting for the following week. But a bad December siege of the flu in the Carey household was to push all thoughts of civic projects from Mrs. Carey's mind for many months. "Flu year," she noted tersely at the top of the page in the ledger where she kept meticulous yearly lists of Christmas gifts. The somber 1924 holiday season ended, but the malevolent effects of influenza continued. Martha Stewart Carey, Mrs. Carey's oldest daughter, who had, for many years, been a principal supporter of Christamore settlement house, was stricken in late February. Ten days later she died, two days before her forty-fifth birthday.

By the end of April, however, Mrs. Carey was ready to turn her attention again to the new museum, and the organizational committee gathered at her home at 1150 North Meridian on April 20, 1925. Several important decisions were made. First, it was decided that the name of the group would be the Children's Museum Association of Indianapolis. Second, the committee decided that the Children's Museum would be an independent body; it would, however, solicit the aid and cooperation of the schools, Indianapolis Foundation and other organizations. (Thirty-two members of Woman's Rotary had already signed up as charter members.)

After some discussion, it was agreed that the material in the new museum should not be limited in scope, but should be informational and of interest to children, and that the viewpoint of the child should be considered in selecting equipment and installations. As to the question of "where," committee members decided only that it was a necessity to have the museum in an open space or park with recreation space for the children.

A subcommittee of three (Coleman, Dalman and Miss Fitch) was appointed to develop a plan of organization and to draft a constitution. By the next general committee meeting a month later, the subcommittee, after meeting three times, was ready with a tentative outline of a constitution and bylaws. In a May 16, 1925 letter, the American Association of Museums formally welcomed the new group into membership (dues, $5 annually). The pace was picking up.

At the group's second public meeting, June 1, 1925, at the John Herron Art Institute, attendance was nearly double that of the first meeting six months earlier. Dalman, who had taken the draft of the constitution and bylaws to attorney Fred Bates Johnson to be checked, read the documents to the assembled museum supporters. Among the provisions: dues for adult voting members would be $1, for junior members (under 21), twenty-five cents; there would be a nine-member board of trustees and a five-member junior executive committee which would consult with the senior board.

But the evening's most important business was the election of the board of trustees. The nominating committee (Coleman and MacLean) presented nine names, five women and four men: Mrs. Carey, Miss Browning, Miss Fitch, Miss Henley, Dalman, Mrs. G.H.A. Clowes, Dwight Ritter, Edgar Evans and Hugh McK. Landon. The slate was elected. The Children's Museum Association had its first board of trustees—almost.

The election had been on Monday, and the board's first meeting was scheduled for June 3, two nights later, again at Mrs. Carey's. By then there had already been some attrition. Evans and Landon had "declined to serve," it was announced. Named instead were Coleman and Indianapolis architect Kurt

Vonnegut. (It may well have been a fortunate substitution. Though Landon's Indianapolis Foundation influence probably would have been helpful, Vonnegut, in particular, proved to be an indefatigable worker during his many years on the museum board.)

So there it was, the museum's first board of trustees. Its members represented not only money and contacts (four of the nine were listed in the current year's *Indianapolis Society Blue Book*) but also the city's cultural and educational community. Mrs. Carey was elected board president; Dalman and Miss Henley, first and second vice presidents; and Dwight Ritter, an Indianapolis businessman, treasurer.

At this Wednesday meeting there was something else promising in the balmy June night air—news of a possible, temporary location for the museum.

CHAPTER THREE
A Gift for the Children

It was time, Mrs. John W. Schmidt had decided in the late 1880s, to move the family home to Indianapolis' north side, away from the vicinity of her husband's brewery. The three-story, Neo-Jacobean brick home which her husband built for her at the corner of Fourteenth Street and North Delaware was imposing indeed. It had a third-floor ballroom, porte-cochere and beautiful, expansive grounds covering nearly a fourth of a city block. Even the barn/carriage house building at the rear of the property was externally attractive. It, too, was a vivid red brick, with the same bands of limestone trim as the main house.

Joseph Schaf, also a brewer, purchased the house in 1905, and for many years the house was the scene of much Schaf-family gaiety. At the elaborate, much-talked-about wedding of Alice Schaf, there was dancing in the ballroom and the caterers operated out of the little carriage house, effectively lighted for the occasion. In time the Schafs, too, moved, and the big house, no longer a private home, was occupied briefly by the Indiana College of Music and Fine Arts. In 1923, the ladies of the Propylaeum, in need of new quarters for club functions, purchased the home and, along with it, the two-story building at the rear and to the south of the main house. With the passing of horses and hay and other carriage house appurtenances, the small building was now sometimes just called the garage.

For several years, the Little Theatre Society used the stable/barn/garage as a workshop, but in 1925, the 10-year-old theatrical group was moving into its new playhouse at Eighteenth and Alabama (where it would change its name to Civic Theatre). This would leave vacant the carriage house, Children's Museum board members were told at their June 3 meeting. It would make a fine temporary location, board members decided, and the new museum association began paying rent on the property July 1, 1925.

Even before it had a location, the new museum had attracted attention in town. Laura A. Smith, *Indianapolis Star* columnist, for instance, was giving the new endeavor steady, if saccharine, attention: "Every day something very nice, very sweet is being planned for little Johnnie and Mary Indianapolis. Now it's hurrah for the children's museum—the latest thing on the tapis. . . . I forget just when it was that Mrs. John N. Carey first told me of the fine plan . . ."

Miss Fitch had gone to see the Brooklyn Children's Museum early in the summer of 1926, and shortly afterwards, while on vacation in the East, columnist Smith decided she, too, should make the Brooklyn pilgrimage. "Miss Indianapolis knows full well why I wanted to take in that institution," she wrote coyly in a late-July feature story. "Have we not a children's museum of our own looming up amid rainbow skies in the near horizon?" The subway ride to the museum was, she confided to her readers, "hot, noisy, gassy, uncomfortable." The museum itself, though, delighted her, even if she was unable to meet its vacationing curator-in-chief, Anna Billings Gallup, who "brought the live coal from her museum which lighted the fire of enthusiasm for our Indianapolis children's museum."

With Brooklyn's Adams mansion undoubtedly in mind, Mrs. Carey was dropping hints, via newspaper stories, that the Indianapolis museum would certainly like to acquire an old family home in the city, one with a historic background, if possible, "with a lawn for the children to rest upon." However, if the "live coal" in Brooklyn and its spark out in Indiana had the same idea about an ideal location, they had different approaches to starting collections.

When it first started, the Brooklyn Children's Museum, with the financial and organizational backing of the Brooklyn Institute of Arts and Sciences, had purchased an already-existing natural history collection as a beginning nucleus, disdaining cast-off items from the Brooklyn Central Museum. ("What is not good enough for adults is certainly far less suitable for children," said institute trustees indignantly.) In contrast, without any comparable financial backing, the new Indianapolis museum was enthusiastically accepting a cheerful hodgepodge of items in its temporary headquarters in the Propylaeum carriage house.

One of the first donations was a large, mounted porcupine fish, given by the visual education department of the city schools. Little Volinda Lewis, one of Mrs. Carey's granddaughters, gave an arrowhead. Miss Fitch donated Italian tiles, which, she reported, were found in a lava stream still hot three months after an eruption. There were snowshoes from Canada, Dutch costumes, a bottle full of sand from the Holy Land. But in addition to curios and tourist knick-knacks, the tiny museum was also beginning to acquire some truly "museum quality" items. There were, for instance, Pre-Columbian Inca pieces from Mr. and Mrs. James B. Gaylord, including a fine stone hammer unearthed in a copper mine and a large, round, ceramic jar which Mrs. Gaylord had carefully carried on horseback thirty miles from an ancient Inca village in northern Chile to the closest railroad station.

The carriage house was being rented on a month-by-month basis for $35 a month ($40 for months when heat was needed). But even with warm-weather rates, by early October the museum was still three months in arrears on its rent. There were 115 senior members and 11 junior members from whom $57.50 in membership fees had so far been collected (an additional $61.25 was still owed). Plans, nevertheless, went optimistically forward. The formal opening of the museum was to be before December 1, if possible, and in the meantime, two weekends in mid-October were being announced as special days when people could bring by more contributions.

At a luncheon meeting in the Propylaeum in late October, Dalman gave his fellow trustees some hard facts that undoubtedly did not have a salutary effect upon digestions. In order to pay the overdue rent, secure a curator, buy cases and organize the material for a December opening, five thousand members were needed—at once. Following lunch, the trustees adjourned to visit their new museum out in back.

Trustee Vonnegut had been put in charge of establishing a program of junior memberships. It was decided that membership buttons would be just the ticket to attract the interest of the city's youngsters. But something else, it was decided, needed to be done to represent the new museum graphically to the community.

One day in late fall Vonnegut walked into the craft room in a small frame building at the rear of the old house occupied by Orchard School. As a parent of students at the school and as a member of the board, he was a familiar visitor. He handed some blueprints to the school's shop, crafts and nature study teacher, a blond young man recently graduated from Butler, Hillis Howie. The blueprints showed a sea horse between the initials CM and under a crown or wave design. Why a sea horse? A theory is that Vonnegut thought the unusual creature would intrigue children and make them curious to learn more about the museum. Also, there had recently been two sea horses in the Orchard School aquarium. Could Howie, Vonnegut wanted to know, saw out of wood a small sea horse like the ones on the drawings? It was to be used for a sign for the new Children's Museum. Howie, of course, like all other Orchard teachers, had already heard much about the proposed museum from Mrs. Carey, the school's "patron saint," and from Orchard headmistress Faye Henley, museum board member. It was an easy request for the competent young craftsman. Within a few hours the sea horse was done. It was about eight inches long, made of half-inch oak. Soon it was dangling from the sign over the door of the Propylaeum carriage house, swaying saucily in the early winter breezes.

But the big need was inside the building. Someone had to bring order to the growing pile of donations laid about on dusty tables in the carriage house. A year earlier, E. Y. Guernsey had read a paper before the Indiana Historical Commission, describing how to build up a museum. Guernsey, a 42-

Mrs. John N. Carey, as painted by Wayman Adams.
Bass photo

Other founders of the Children's Museum were Murray Dalman (above left), Eliza Browning (above right, later photo), Florence Fitch (below left) and Faye Henley (below right, later photo).

Photos: Dalman, Indianapolis Star-News; Browning, Indianapolis-Marion County Public Library; Henley, Clem C. Voorhis.

The carriage house behind the Indianapolis Propylaeum was the museum's first home.
Children's Museum photo

The first newspaper photo about the museum appeared in late October 1925, showing two neighborhood boys, Billy (rear) and George Wildhack, looking at items being collected in the carriage house. Indianapolis News photo

A sea horse was designed as the museum's emblem by trustee Kurt Vonnegut, Sr. (above).

A walnut bench (or settle), donated by Mrs. John N. Carey, was one of the museum's early acquisitions.
Indianapolis Star photo

year-old Bedford, Indiana, businessman and landowner, was becoming a productive and respected Indiana archaeologist. He had published an archaeological survey of Lawrence County and had worked for the Museum of Natural History in Los Angeles. (He was also soon to begin a twenty-year career in the Indiana state legislature.) Coleman and Miss Henley suggested that he be contacted about coming to Indianapolis for a few days each week to get things ready for the December opening. Guernsey came up to Indianapolis on November 27 to meet with the trustees and to have a look at the small museum. The decision was made to keep the museum at its present location, but the December 1 opening date was postponed. Instead, it was decided to call the week of December 7 Museum Week, a week of "organized effort to secure museum material and equipment, so that we may open our museum formally about January 1," as a letter, sent out to civic organizations by the board, explained.

A key part of Museum Week was an approach, through school children and their families, to the community for support. Fortunately, strong support for the new museum was developing from the public school administration. This was probably in good measure a result of having two school administrators (Dalman and Miss Fitch) among the museum's original organizers, as well as having the support of others of influence within the school system. Miss McClellan, for instance, was chairman of the Children's Museum natural history advisory committee; Flora Drake, an assistant superintendent, was among those giving speeches about the museum to special groups in the community.

At the beginning of Museum Week (and with official permission of the school office), teachers in classrooms across the city read to their pupils a letter signed by Mrs. Carey. "Did you ever visit a museum? Was it not interesting? How would you like for the children of Indianapolis to have a museum of their very own?" asked the letter. The museum would be "a lasting Christmas gift to Indianapolis children, where admission will be free to all." And here is where their part came in, the school children were told. "There are in the homes of Indianapolis thousands of things, sometimes stored away and almost forgotten, that would be very interesting to all of us. Will you not help us find those things? . . . Talk to your parents about it. . . . Nothing is too great or too small for the museum. The only question asked is, 'Will it be of interest to children?' "

Though the adults in the community might be waiting for the official, formal opening of the museum, the children—the museum's most important audience—weren't. Those in the neighborhood had been dropping by since fall to look at the growing collection of fascinating things spread out on table tops. And now Mrs. Carey extended an invitation to all children throughout the city. Though the formal opening would be in January, she said in a Museum Week letter, "You are invited to visit the museum at 126 East Fourteenth any time this week . . ."

Among the material brought in during museum week was the entire Orchard School museum—eight boxes full of treasures. At Miss Henley's suggestion, the children had been bringing to school items which were then displayed in sectional bookcases in the former front room of Orchard's house on North Meridian. And now they were going to share what they had collected with the rest of the city's boys and girls.

In the days following Museum Week, developments occurred rapidly, affecting not only the date, but the place of the museum's formal opening. For one thing, Guernsey had taken ill and returned to Bedford. It was not going to be possible to hire him as full-time director (if, indeed, that was ever the intention). Instead, a temporary director would have to be considered. At the December 16 board meeting, there was still talk of painting walls and doing whatever else was necessary to get the museum ready for a holiday season opening in the carriage house. However, at the conclusion of the board meeting, off went a committee from the board to see the city's mayor about a new location for the museum.

The museum contingent (Mrs. Carey and Coleman) had an important ally when they were ushered into Mayor Lew Shank's third-floor City Hall office. Accompanying them was Mrs. Shank. Could the museum, they asked, please have some ground for a building at Thirtieth and Boulevard Place? The mayor instead offered the use of the new shelter house at the city's Garfield Park, and Mrs. Shank took the committee out to the south-side park to have a look.

Two days later, on December 18, the results of the visits to the mayor and the park were reported to the rest of the board at a special meeting. (Ironically, Guernsey had just finished a detailed report, dated December 17, which described the Fourteenth Street location as "admirable"—if the building were put in proper condition—and recommended specific things to be done to put it in that condition.) The following week, Mrs. Shank and the museum committee, this time augmented by Vonnegut, met with the park board. The Garfield Park location had several points in its favor: there would be no painting or remodeling costs; adjacent to the rooms the museum would be occupying was a spacious auditorium which would be available for special programs; and—best news of all to the impecunious organization—rent, heat, light and janitorial services would all be provided free.

On December 24, as Indianapolis households finished wrapping packages and hanging shiny ornaments on fragrant evergreen trees, the park board voted to let the museum move into the south wing of the Garfield Park building. The Children's Museum had a new location. A Christmas gift, indeed, for the children of Indianapolis.

CHAPTER FOUR
New Home in the Park

Sled tracks criss-crossed the hill on the east side of the long, brick building which sat, commandingly, atop the high ridge in Garfield Park. There had been snow the night before—not much, only about an inch and a half. But for serious sledders with an afternoon off from school, that was enough.

By midafternoon, even though the temperature had crawled up from the chilly five degrees of the night before, it was still cold. The sledders who came stamping into the Garfield Park Community House to warm up had much to look at this particular Friday afternoon. Something called a Children's Museum had moved into the building two weeks earlier, and this afternoon, from 3 to 5 p.m., was its special, formal opening.

The park's 4-year-old community house, a handsome building with high-pitched gambrel roof of slate, had been called "a showplace of the midwest" by local newspapers. It had a large room in the center, two stories high with French doors running along both sides. At either end of this room were two smaller, single-story wings. It was the wing on the south end that had been taken over by the museum and its dolls, spinning wheels, Russian washboard, mounted butterflies and waist-high cases filled with Indian relics.

The two-hour Friday afternoon opening was a great success—even if only four of the museum's nine trustees attended. There was, in fact, "a mob," Florence Fitch happily reported in a letter to Mrs. Carey, who was out of town. William Herschell, a popular local newspaper writer and poet, was scheduled to present a brief program of poetry readings. Throughout the afternoon, as the tall oaks in a grove at the south end of the building cast lengthening shadows in the winter sun, between four hundred and five hundred people milled about inside, viewing the museum exhibits.

The next afternoon, an enthusiastic, full-page feature article (with pictures) about the new museum, written by Herschell, appeared in the *Indianapolis News* ("No local movement in recent years has gathered momentum and enthusiasm comparable with that now centering in the Children's Museum of Indianapolis."). After more than fourteen months of meetings, plans, delays and a last-minute change in location, to have the museum officially open must have been a relief, indeed, to those who had worked so hard to bring it into being.

This formal opening was held only sixteen days after the museum had been packed up and moved from the Propylaeum carriage house to Garfield Park. The January 6 move, apparently completed in one day, was supervised by J. Arthur MacLean, director of the Herron Art Institute and, though not yet a trustee, chairman of the Children's Museum's museum relations committee. (MacLean's interests included not only fine art but archaeology; later in 1926 and in 1927 he would direct the first modern archaeological excavation undertaken in Indiana, at the Albee Mound in Sullivan County.)

On January 7, the day after the collections were moved, the museum's board of trustees held a special meeting at the community house, at which it was announced that school principals and other administrators, plus the mayor and park department officials, were being invited to an afternoon reception the following week to see the new facility. The museum was now open weekday and Sunday afternoons and all day Saturday, Dalman told school principals in a January 18 notice. And the reason the fledgling museum could now be open was that a curator had been found and had started to work on January 10. He was a 19-year-old Butler University student named Stewart Springer.

Springer had been first brought to the board's attention as a possible, temporary curator for the new museum by Rousseau McClellan, the Shortridge High School natural science teacher; he had been one of her former pupil-assistants. He also came with high recommendations from the Boy Scout executive office and the Culver (Indiana) summer Woodcraft School where he had taught. "He is recognized as an authority on snakes, having made an intensive study of various species and the variation within the species," reported the museum committee which engaged him. For his twenty-eight hours of work at the museum each week he was to be paid $17.

Springer had started out at Butler in pre-med and then switched to biology. Mornings he attended classes at Butler's campus in Irvington, then traveled, usually by streetcar, to Garfield Park and his new museum job. Occasionally his sister would let him drive her car, a Maxwell, to work. But that was only if he made sure he picked her up at the Severin Hotel, where she was the cellist in a dinner-hour string trio, and rushed her to either the Murat Theatre or English's, where she often played in the pit orchestras. If the borrowed Maxwell added a touch of importance to the young curator's arrival at Garfield Park, it also added some headaches. It had no antifreeze, so on the frequent, very cold winter afternoons, Springer would have to drain out the water from the radiator when he parked, then bring out a teakettle of water to refill it when it was time to leave.

On a Saturday afternoon in late February, one month after its formal opening, the new museum presented its first educational program. Arranged by Miss Fitch, it, too, was a great success. As about six hundred people watched, a tiny, 70-year-old Danish woman, who hadn't used a spinning wheel since she left Denmark six years earlier, pushed tirelessly on the foot treadle of the museum's small wheel. Nearby stood her proud, 12-year-old grandson, translating into English her words of explanation. Also on the program were three small children from School Thirty-five using hand looms. Old coverlets were on display with other early American items: a fireplace cooking spider, a colonial table, a combination settee and rocker, a bed warmer. The day's only disappointment came when another, larger spinning wheel failed to work properly because of wool that wasn't in the proper condition.

Springer had no exact idea of how his duties at the museum would develop. But, given his interests, he hoped that many projects concerning natural history would be involved. To his disappointment, much of his time seemed to be spent in cataloging dolls, dolls, dolls. However, there were opportunities to work with Boy Scouts on bird study merit badges, using the museum's study collection of bird skins. And there were the visitors to talk to, adults as well as the neighborhood children. Some of the visitors were as interesting as the exhibits they came to inspect—a Civil War veteran, for instance, who spent much of the afternoon patiently answering Springer's questions about the campaigns in which he had participated.

Springer was given $5 a month petty cash to meet incidental museum expenses. He suspected that the trustees of the financially hard-pressed new organization were sometimes meeting expenses out of their own pockets. As an economy measure, the telephone was even taken out after a month's monitoring of calls showed that it was being used more by park employees than for museum business.

By the end of February, more than 600 items—431 loans and 200 gifts—had been cataloged. They came in all sizes and shapes. A small, live alligator was donated to the museum, as was the large, mounted head of an American elk. The latter was donated by trustee Vonnegut in the name of his three children, Bernard, Alice and Kurt Jr. Vonnegut suggested it be positioned over a fireplace in the Garfield Park building.

Between fifteen hundred and sixteen hundred people had visited the museum during its first month. However, the museum, in its south-side location, was turning out to be a bit off the track for many of the trustees. They didn't pass it on their way from north-side homes and apartments to downtown offices. They didn't pass it on shopping trips downtown to Charlie Mayer's or Ayres or Block's, or on the way to programs at the art institute. No longer was it possible to have luncheon board meetings at the Propylaeum, then walk across the lawn to see how things were going. Instead, board meetings were generally being held downtown at the Board of Trade building—far removed from Garfield Park both psychologically and visually, if not in actual miles.

Even though the committee which had selected Springer had been very specific in listing his duties (at least in the report that it had turned into the board), the new young curator felt a bit adrift, without any definite guidance, unsure of the direction the trustees wished the museum to follow. Yet they, too, he realized, were feeling their way, and a couple of them did regularly drive out to help move furniture or sort through new donations. The appointment committee had, as a matter of fact, specifically recommended that, in order "not to confuse the appointee by too many directions," he should receive directions only from Miss Henley, the chairman of the committee which had appointed him, and Dalman, the board's acting president (Mrs. Carey was out of town much of the time). They undoubtedly did not realize that their young employee interpreted this limited contact as lack of interest and appreciation.

At the May board meeting, it was announced that Springer's plans for the summer necessitated his leaving the museum before the July 1 date originally agreed upon. Before the end of the month, however, another curator had been lined up: Arthur B. Carr, whose father was a cousin of E. Y. Guernsey's. "I think Mr. Carr will do very well in bringing the physical aspects of the Children's Museum up to a point where it will be the pride and admiration of those associated with it," wrote MacLean (now a member of the board) to Miss Fitch. Beginning May 30, 1926, Carr plunged into bringing order to what he saw as the neglectful operation of the museum. Cases were unlocked, file cards were gone, acquisition data was incomplete or nonexistent and exhibit material was missing, a very irritated Carr reported to the board.

The museum's first curator was, in truth, a talented naturalist whose real interest was in studying snakes in Borneo or other field work, not in indoor cataloging. (Springer published his first technical paper the following year in *Proceedings of the Indiana Academy of Science, 1927.*) Now, however, the Children's Museum had acquired as curator a true, passionate collector and organizer who took on all aspects of museum operation with energy and enthusiasm, if not formal museum training.

Arthur Carr was 55 years old, slim, gray-haired, professorial in appearance. He was graduated with a degree in pharmacy (and an excellent academic record) from Purdue University, where he was president of the pharmacy senior class of 1895. But though his profession was pharmacy, his passion was amateur archaeology. Like Guernsey, Carr (a native of Henryville), had grown up in southern Indiana's Clark County, where there were lots of interesting Indian artifacts for a boy to kick up in freshly plowed fields after a rain. His father, James L. Carr, had been an enthusiastic amateur collector, and in his village store, he would often trade candy or pocket knives or a pair of suspenders for interesting Indian relics that farm boys would bring in. The items in his collection eventually numbered in the thousands. (It was the senior Carr and his hobby which first got Guernsey interested in archaeology as well.) Carr was also influenced by the collection of a friend of his father's, William W. Borden, of nearby New Providence. After making his fortune in Colorado mining, Borden had returned to Indiana and had opened a school and a museum. Like these men, Arthur Carr had become a serious collector. (As a matter of fact, in his report to the museum five months earlier, Guernsey had called Arthur Carr's collection of artifacts "one of the best archaeological collections in the state" and had recommended the Children's Museum try to obtain it.) At Carr's drugstore, on the corner of Nineteenth and Alabama in Indianapolis, the front window and many of the cases inside were filled with displays of various specimens, which brought in fascinated neighborhood kids. To give such a man a museum to organize was like giving the honey jar to a bear.

Carr had sold his drugstore in 1922, but he still continued to work at least part-time as a pharmacist, even during his first years running the museum. But even with a more appropriate hand at the helm, there were still shoals aplenty for the museum. Money, as always, was one. Even though Carr was, for the time being, donating his services to the museum, the museum was in debt, with no funds in sight, as the end of 1926 approached.

In addition, the Garfield Park location was producing some headaches. Even during Springer's tenure, several ladies in the Garfield Park area had registered their unhappiness that the museum was occupying rooms originally designed as ladies "rest" rooms (rest in the sense of reception rooms or rooms for special women's activities). Also, the ample lawns and play areas of the ideal location, as envisioned by the museum's planners, now appeared to have drawbacks. "I'm not convinced that a Children's Museum, established near a recreation ground or center, is *well* located; for the lure of the playground is intense, and the actual time spent by the children themselves in observation of the instructive material on exhibit, is usually very short," wrote Carr in a monthly report to the board.

Carr was also having some trouble with children in the neighborhood—"rough necks," as he termed them, who mutilated the pages of the guest register, and "ragamuffin youngsters," who broke the glass in a display case as well as damaged trees during one night's rowdy spree. Obviously, it was time to look for a new location.

A special board meeting was held in early November while Mrs. Carey was in town to discuss finances and location. Mrs. Carey, who presided, said she would contribute $100 a year as her membership. A committee of two, board treasurer Ritter and a non-board member, Eugene C. Foster, secretary of the Indianapolis Foundation, was appointed to locate other quarters. (Museum board members had been wooing the foundation for many months without an official pledge of financial support. Instead, the foundation had earlier suggested that the museum get together with the "several" other groups in town also trying to get funds to establish museums.)

The Herron Art Institute was asked if it could take in the new museum, but declined (MacLean was in the process of leaving as director). Ritter unsuccessfully tried to see Mrs. Benjamin Harrison in New York to convince her to sell the North Delaware Street home of the former president to the museum (backed by funds from a patriotic group such as the DAR).

Prices on other large, old houses in Indianapolis were investigated, but nothing developed.

All tiptoed gingerly around one obvious solution to the location—Mrs. Carey. Orchard School was moving from Mrs. Carey's property at 5050 North Meridian; the big, Carey family house at 1150 North Meridian was empty much of the time. (Mrs. Carey, when she wasn't out of town, was spending more time at Haverway since John Carey's death the previous spring.) Yet this didn't seem like the time to approach her, said MacLean in a letter to Dalman, inasmuch as she had "insisted on the vacation" of the property Orchard had been using in order to get her affairs "into more liquid form."

The park board was just as anxious as the museum board to see the spinning wheels, rock specimens and arrowheads move from Garfield Park, and by early 1927, a new location became imperative. One year after its auspicious opening, the museum had more than two thousand junior members and five hundred adult members—and no home. With no place else to turn, the board at last hastily contacted Mrs. Carey in Florida. Her telegram giving the board permission to move the museum into her North Meridian Street home had already arrived and the move was underway by the time a carefully worded letter was officially received from the park board: "We will be very glad if you can find other quarters to carry on this splendid work. Trusting this letter will not be misunderstood, as we appreciate what your work means. . . ."

Mrs. Carey's house was expected to provide only temporary shelter for her museum waif; the trustees continued to investigate other property. Nevertheless, a month after the move, Carr was again ready for visitors. On Saturday, April 16, 1927, the day before Easter, after three days of special openings for members, the Children's Museum opened to the public at 1150 North Meridian. It was to be the museum's address for the next nineteen years.

CHAPTER FIVE
1150 North Meridian

The big old house at 1150 North Meridian was used to children and good times.

Excited Carey grandchildren had trooped through its halls singing "Oh say, don't you know it is Christmas," as they marched on Christmas Day to the front parlor, its doors mysteriously closed for the past week. With drama, the doors were opened to reveal an always-tall, always-dazzling Christmas tree. In earlier days, the same rooms, fragrant with roses, chandeliers draped with Southern smilax and pink crepe, had been filled with out-of-town visitors and Indianapolis gentry bringing good wishes to a Carey daughter making her debut. In the library, discreetly screened by palms, an orchestra had played.

John and Mary Carey were not the house's first owners. It had been built in 1873 by John M. Lord, a wealthy attorney, Mexican War veteran and president of Indianapolis Rolling Mill, which had made its fortune in railroad iron. Within a few years the house was sold to a successful stove and hollowware merchant named Robert L. McOuat, and then again in 1887, to Robert B. F. Peirce, an attorney, railroad executive and former U.S. Congressman. Here, it was said, Mrs. Peirce had entertained many turn-of-the-century theatrical greats—Otis Skinner, Edwin Booth, Ellen Terry, Julia Marlowe.

The three-story house, with its ballroom, mansard roof and long, stone-capped windows, was purchased in 1903 by John and Mary Carey in the twenty-fourth year of their marriage. Some of its rooms had sixteen-foot ceilings and graceful bays, and there was carved mahogany paneling in the dining room. The renowned landscaping firm of Frederick Law Olmstead (he designed Central Park and the grounds of Vanderbilt's Biltmore estate) was brought to Indianapolis to landscape the property. The firm planned a semiformal garden in the rear with pergola and lion's head wall fountain. The mansion (thirty-five rooms, some said) was obviously a house for entertaining, and invitations bearing the silver Carey crest (a swan afloat on the Latin inscription *Virtute —Excerpta*) were often in Indianapolis mailboxes. In addition to formal parties, there were evenings of charades (a particular favorite of Mrs. Carey's), bridge, mahjong and rehearsals of Dramatic Club productions.

It was the scene of more serious functions as well. The Gen. Arthur St. Clair chapter of the Daughters of the American Revolution was organized in its front rooms, and the committee to select a state flag for Indiana (Mrs. Carey was chairman) cast a majority vote for the torch and stars design at a meeting in the house. John Carey had his areas of philanthropic interest as well. The house's long dining room and front parlors were the scenes of annual banquets for the Young Men's Christian Association and committee meetings at which preliminary work was done to organize Methodist Hospital.

It was into a few, first-floor rooms of these splendid quarters that Carr moved the Children's Museum's growing collection, attempting to arrange things into "somewhat credible exhibits," he reported to the board. "The possibilities for display of material, and the developing of special exhibits is limited only by time, help and funds."

Ah yes, funds. The location problem might be temporarily solved, but there was still no money. It bothered Carr that board treasurer Ritter was paying expenses out of his own pocket, though Carr himself would do the same thing throughout the early, lean period. And there was generally not enough money to pay Carr the $100 a month salary he was now supposed to be receiving. "Is it fair to those who have labored to 'put this thing over' that there should be less than wholehearted cooperation from, or among the members of the Board and . . . but a feeble effort to place the institution on a sound

financial basis?" he sternly lectured the board in another report. "Is it fair to Mr. Ritter, to expect or allow him to under-
write our expenses for last year, this year, or in the future?" A
few months later Mrs. Carey offered the museum the income
($360 annually) from an advertising signboard that had been
erected on the south edge of the property.

About other aspects of the museum (the impact it could
have on children of all kinds, for instance), Carr was a bit
happier. A group of small boys who played around the museum always made a point of washing their hands at a nearby
filling station before asking to come inside the museum, prov-
ing, Carr told the trustees, that "cultural things have a dis-
tinctly elevating influence." However, Carr admitted, in one
instance he might have overdone attempts to make the museum seem fascinating. He had told a group of boys about
finding, by accident, two secret panels or compartments in the
house. In the days following he began hearing strange tapping
sounds. When he investigated, he found boys on their knees
thumping panels and examining out-of-the-way corners in the
big, old house.

Newspaper writer Laura Smith was delighted to have the
museum in its new setting, but she was all for renaming it.
"The name museum undoubtedly rattles like dry bones in the
minds of the majority, so I prefer the term wonder house."

With the museum gradually looking more museum-like,
the flow of exhibit material increased. One exhibit even came
chugging and snorting up under its own one-cylinder, four-
cycle power: the horseless carriage built by Charles Black,
which many in Indianapolis liked to think was the first
gasoline-powered vehicle in America. Black was a local carriage
maker with a shop at the corner of Pennsylvania and Maryland
Streets. Though the "first in America" title (Black claimed he
drove it in 1891) and the exact pedigree of some of its components were later widely disputed, it was undoubtedly one of
the early cars driven around under its own power on Indianapolis streets. His family decided to lend it to the new museum where it could be put on display.

But as pleased as Carr was to acquire things, he was also
eager to see the museum become more than just a repository.

If the museum were to "become a really vital factor in the educational system of the community," he told the trustees, there would need to be programs and activities in natural history and other areas to "stimulate in the citizens of tomorrow, the desire to investigate and think for themselves." So Carr, who was already greeting visitors, giving tours, designing and arranging exhibits and labeling and cataloging new arrivals, added planning programs and activities to his list. And still there was work to be done. Publicity had to be supplied to the newspapers and contacts needed to be made with civic clubs and businesses which might be cajoled into giving financial support. Carr obviously could not do it all.

In January 1928, a 28-year-old Indianapolis native, married and the mother of a 4-year-old daughter, was hired on a trial, three-month basis to take care of these latter concerns. Her name was Grace Blaisdell Golden. Before her marriage, Grace Blaisdell had been educational secretary for the local tuberculosis association; after her marriage she had done some part-time public relations work and free-lance newspaper writing. Either at that time or earlier she had become a friend of Agnes McCulloch Hanna, who had become a museum trustee in 1927, and who also did some newspaper feature writing. It was probably Mrs. Hanna who first brought Grace Golden to the museum's attention. In April the board voted to hire Mrs. Golden for two more months, "because of her ability." By the end of the year, she and Carr had produced the first *Sea Horse Bulletin,* a publication for young members.

One of the facets of the museum's operation in which it took particular pride was its junior board of school pupils. Though there were five other United States cities with children's museums, said the *Indianapolis Star,* "ours is the only one having a junior board of directors chosen from school zones in the city to act as trustees to plan . . . museum activities."

The junior board, established by the museum's constitution, had evolved from the junior service clubs organized by Vonnegut at individual schools. Participation on the board was used as an incentive to increase the percentage of pupils at each school who paid their twenty-five cents and received their sea horse buttons during the annual January membership campaign. The five schools with the highest percentage of members named representatives to the board.

Though there was, of course, a limited amount of actual museum planning these school youngsters could participate in, they did get to do such things as be hosts at the annual meeting (one year in Japanese costume to promote a current Japanese exhibit) and assist with collecting material for museum exhibits. For instance, late in the 1928 school year, children were encouraged to bring in items from their homes for exhibits at their individual schools. From these exhibits Carr and the trustees would select pieces to be used in summer exhibits at the "main" museum. One of the interesting things the museum organizers had learned after the first collection appeal aimed directly to school pupils (Mrs. Carey's 1925 Museum Week letter) was that children from what the newspapers called "the foreign quarter" responded well, apparently proud to share items from their families' Old World past. This time Carr told the newspapers he was particularly anxious to get "foreign material which . . . may be found in immigrant homes." Soon, such things as a German vase and a Scandinavian pillow (for teaching children how to make pillow lace) were added to the museum's collection.

It was items like these which were creating the nucleus of what would become the museum's strong, social culture collection. In truth, though, all three of the people who had done curatorial chores for the museum (Carr, Springer and Guernsey) were more interested in natural history and thus, perhaps not surprisingly, were more thorough in cataloging a rock specimen than a smoothing iron.

For tiny children with no interest in either geology or social culture, Carr had put together a tiny, wooded scene of *Goldilocks and the Three Bears* complete with tiny bowls, a broken chair and three bears from Switzerland. This scene joined the growing number of "classified exhibits" which now filled twenty-two rooms in the museum, a half-heartedly anonymous letter to the editor (signed A.B.C.) proudly pointed out to readers of the *Indianapolis News*. There was a marine room, pioneer room, Japanese room, archaeology room, natural history room and a small library with books and magazines on nature study. Two large collections had been lent—the T.H. Parry collection of early American guns, and many items, including an inlaid Senate gavel used by United States vice president during Grover Cleveland's first term, Thomas A. Hendricks, who was from Indianapolis.

To put together the settings for some of the Japanese material, Carr had scavenged scraps of cigar boxes, coal and stones from the museum's yard. It was a necessary economy at the destitute museum. By the fall of 1928, not only were the museum's financial troubles still unsolved, but it was losing one of its energetic early leaders. Dalman, who had taken over as president of the board of trustees in May 1927 (Mrs. Carey was named honorary president), was moving to Chicago to become an educational consultant for an architectural firm.

The board struggled on, with Miss Henley as acting president. Briefly there were high hopes that two special fund-raising events would help provide some much-needed funds. Both were disappointments. "Simba," a movie of a Martin and Johnson African expedition, was to play at English's; in exchange for helping to promote the evening, the museum was to receive any profits over $10,000. Not surprisingly—with a minimum like that—there apparently weren't any, despite Miss Fitch's heroic efforts to get out attendance. (Belatedly, the film's owner and the theater management did make a $100 donation to the museum.)

The second fund raiser involved promoting November concerts by the nation's favorite bandmaster, John Philip Sousa, for which the museum was to receive 5 percent of the returns. The concerts were to be held at Cadle Tabernacle, a large mock-Spanish-style downtown auditorium used for conventions, concerts and religious gatherings featuring the likes of Billy Sunday and Aimee Semple McPherson. In appreciation for the museum's work and interest, Sousa announced that he was sending the museum an eighteen-inch-high silver loving cup, which was put on display downtown in a window at L.S. Ayres the week before the concerts. Museum trustees, in turn, announced that the loving cup would go to the school which won the museum's next annual membership drive.

Interestingly enough, a few weeks later the rules changed a bit. The Sousa Cup, it was announced, would go to the *public school* with the greatest percentage of members, and another cup, to be called the Founder's Cup, donated by Mrs. John N. Carey, would go to the winning private or parochial school. When the last bars of "The Stars and Stripes Forever" had faded away, the museum had not earned much money, but there had been publicity and, of course, the loving cup—or cups. But loving cups don't pay coal bills. With only $133.50 in the bank, the board finally voted to borrow $762 from the bank to pay its debts.

Things, however, were about to improve. New board president Kurt Vonnegut announced a pull-out-the-stops community membership drive, with businessman Warren B. Oakes, a member of the museum advisory board, as chairman. Helped by $100 life memberships from community leaders, the month-long campaign was very successful. The bank note was immediately paid.

Another bright spot was the evaluation of the museum in Eugene T. Lies' 1929 book, *The Leisure of a People*. The book, a survey conducted under the auspices of the Council of Social Agencies, analyzed the recreational facilities available in Indianapolis. Though he had harsh things to say about much in Indianapolis, his comments about the museum (to which he devoted a whole chapter) were most enthusiastic. "The Children's Museum is one of the most charming institutions found in Indianapolis by this Survey. Its founders deserve a high place in the regard of the people of this city."

With the museum at last financially in the black (at least for the time being), modest plans for expansion were made and Carr's salary was raised to $150 a month. One December morning in 1930, Dr. Clark Wissler, curator-in-chief of anthropology at the American Museum of Natural History in New York City, who was in Indianapolis to address the Indiana Historical Society, came to visit the Children's Museum. He asked many questions and commented favorably upon the material. He even publicly praised the museum in his remarks before the historical group, saying (as Carr later remembered his words), "I want to express my earnest approval of the work which is being done in that institution, and recommend that the museum receive the hearty support it deserves." It wasn't likely that Carr would forget those words. To him, they must have been eminently more satisfying than a hundred raises in salary.

CHAPTER SIX
Pot Sherds and Buffalo Skulls

The black Model A station wagon, its once-shiny, varnished, wooden side panels now dull with dust, picked its way slowly across the northern Arizona desert. Inside, a treasure, large, unwieldy and white, rested on the lap of one of the passengers. Once the wagon track was reached, the way would be a bit easier, but there would still be need for care. It was very fragile, this treasure.

The car's destination was a nearby, isolated campsite: a few tents pitched around a large supply truck. A white buffalo skull with sightless black sockets was emblazoned on the truck's rear tarpaulin, and on its front doors, carefully lettered in white, were the group's credentials:

Field Expedition
CHILDREN'S MUSEUM
Indianapolis

As the truck and accompanying station wagons had made the journey from Indiana to Arizona, many who had seen the lettering had misread it. "I didn't know the Field Museum had a boys' expedition," they would say, thinking it was the large, well-known Chicago museum that the group of seventeen boys and their three adult leaders represented. But it was the museum in Indianapolis, not Chicago, that was the destination of these boys and their treasure, a plaster-of-Paris cast of a dinosaur footprint, preserved through the eons by the dry, hot, southwestern sands of the area that later human arrivals called the Painted Desert.

The footprint, the largest of about a dozen tracks discovered in an outcropping of Jurassic sandstone, had three toes, the longest measuring sixteen inches. It would be a splendid specimen for the 1931 Prairie Trek expedition to take back to the museum. Actually, an attempt had been made the year before when the tracks were first discovered by excited Prairie Trekkers. But that summer there hadn't been enough plaster of Paris, and the mixture had been too watery to harden properly. Things looked good, however, for this second try.

Suddenly, the station wagon hit a depression—a thank-you-ma'am, as they were sometimes called—and the boy with the cast on his lap bounced high into the air. As the other boys in the car watched in horror, the flat, white disk landed—and shattered.

The disappointment of an unsuccessful second attempt at bringing the dinosaur print back to Indianapolis was soon blotted out by other activities. There was archaeological work, for instance, on a Pueblo III culture ruin also discovered by the Prairie Trek expedition the year before. The trekkers had been traveling along the old wagon track (a famous trail into Utah used by migrating Mormons) when sharp-eyed boys sitting in the back seat of the station wagon had spotted bits of pottery along the edge of the track. They followed the trail of sherds to the top of a small, nearby mesa. There they also found a tiny seepage, the location of an ancient spring. Sherd Spring Ruin, the Indianapolis party christened the spot, and they began collecting representative examples of the abundant, variously decorated, thousand-year-old pottery fragments.

The 1930 Prairie Trek had been a milestone one, not only because of the discoveries of the dinosaur footprints and Sherd Spring Ruin, but because it was the first year the expedition had been associated with the Children's Museum. Hillis Howie, the young craft and nature study teacher at Orchard, had organized the first Prairie Trek expedition four years earlier in 1926, after hearing about camping trips of the West taken by boys he had known as a counselor at Culver's summer Woodcraft School. Mounting a similar trip had great appeal to the 23-year-old Howie, for it brought together his interests in camping, nature and education. Eight or nine weeks and six thousand miles of "easy, nomad life," the detailed, twenty-three-page prospectus promised parents of possible trekkers, mostly members of the Boy Scout troop which Howie led. Howie expected to take about four boys the first year. Nine boys, at $350 each, signed up to make the trip.

Howie drafted as his assistant Stewart Springer, who had left his job with the Children's Museum a few months earlier. Each man drove one of the expedition's Model Ts, customized with special Martin-Parry "Country Club" bodies with canvas water bags hanging from the rear posts. In addition to boys and tents and other miscellaneous gear, Springer also carried in his car a five-gallon milk can filled with formaldehyde. When the group stopped at night, the boys would scatter through the countryside, returning with all kinds of things—fossils, minerals and sometimes toads and other small amphibians and reptiles to be plopped into Springer's formaldehyde can. Springer showed the boys the rudiments of good zoological field techniques—how to tie on Dennison labels with the date and location of the find, how to make identifications. And to stimulate the boys' interest, he began awarding points, which varied according to how rare or common the specimen. The boy with the most points was to receive, at the end of the trip, a coveted treasure, Springer's machete.

As Howie watched the boys' growing enthusiasm for Springer's project, he realized that these "summer camps on wheels" could be more than sightseeing: here was the potential for sound, scientific education. On future treks boys would choose from among several specialities: mammalogy, ethnology, geology, archaeology, ornithology, herpetology, photography—even journalism. (Boys choosing the last were responsible for sending reports on the expedition back to the *Indianapolis Star*.)

The combination of exuberance and inexperience made the first trek sometimes more of an adventure than anticipated. At House Rock Valley near the Utah-Arizona border, trees were tied to the rear axles of the cars to slow their descent down the steep incline. Wrote Howie a few years later, "I now wonder how we managed to push overloaded Model T Fords

over unimproved roads across the prairies and the Rockies
. . . over the Tetons. . . ."

For the first three summers—1926, 1927 and 1928, "the
Model T summers"—the treks had a decided Scout emphasis.
In 1928, Howie left Orchard School to teach for a year at the
Dalton School in New York City. The following summer, 1929,
Howie was invited to take his Prairie Trek expedition to
England as the official Indianapolis delegation to an inter-
national Scout jamboree. Several things about the jamboree
disillusioned Howie about Scouting (the fancy quarters of some
Scout leaders, for instance), and from then on, the boys of the
Prairie Trek, as Howie put it, no longer wore shorts, but long
dungarees.

In the winter of 1930, Howie, now back in Indianapolis
and at Orchard School, sent a letter to the Children's Museum
board offering to make the trek a museum expedition "to seek
and secure archaeological and natural history exhibits for the
museum." The trustees accepted the offer with enthusiasm,
particularly since the museum's support was to be institutional,
intellectual, even psychological—but not financial. It was a
natural connection, for Howie himself had served on the museum board for a year before going to New York. In the museum yard one morning in July 1930, seventeen boys, felt
patches of the trek's buffalo-skull insignia (made by Howie's
mother) stitched to the front of their cotton flannel sweatshirts,
draped themselves on and around the expedition's 1½-ton
supply truck for an official picture before heading west.

During the following years the museum/trek association
worked well. The boys had an incentive to follow up a specific
interest, to collect and to write up observations. The museum,
its red and white sea horse pennant flying at campsites in
national parks, got good publicity as well as a wide variety of
exhibit material. The cast of the dinosaur footprint finally made
it back safely to Indianapolis after a third try in the summer of
1932. The next summer's finds included two fossilized oreodon
skulls (a prehistoric plains animal about the size of a sheep)
from the South Dakota Badlands. In 1934, the trekkers brought
home to the museum a replica of a whirling-log-design Indian

sand painting. In addition to these spectacular trophies, there were, of course, buckets of pot sherds, pieces of beaver-gnawed aspen wood, preserved specimens of small desert animals, kachina dolls and meteor fragments. The trekkers also helped to collect small mammals for both the Washington National Zoo and the American Museum of Natural History.

The boys were "encouraged" to send home daily post cards, often illustrated, which gave both the young explorers a diary record to keep, and their parents proof that they were still alive. The night before the expedition arrived back at the Children's Museum, one last campfire would be held, usually at Turkey Run State Park, where each boy would be given three minutes to tell what he had gotten from the summer's experience. Nominations were made for the best week, the best day, the best hour and the best five minutes of the eight-week trip. As the young adventurers drifted off to sleep in the warm Hoosier night, their thoughts returned to sunsets at the Grand Canyon and moonlight capture-the-flag games on New Mexican sand dunes. Howie could sometimes be prevailed upon to do his imitation of the eight-hoot call of a barred owl. To the boys' great delight, sometimes out of the black summer night would come eight hoots in answer—from the real thing.

With all this fun and adventure for boys, there was soon interest in having something similar for girls. In 1934, the Turquoise Trail, an expedition for girls, headed west. Its leader was Gordon Thompson, a fellow Orchard School teacher and Howie's assistant on earlier Prairie Treks. He, in turn, was assisted by Howie's wife, Elizabeth, and Mrs. Donald Jameson, a Children's Museum board member and Orchard parent whose two daughters were among the young ladies making the trip. The girls' expedition was not associated with the museum. Though the two groups crossed paths only occasionally, the leaders noticed with amusement that the boys' noses got a bit out of joint at the idea that girls could do even reasonably well at some of the western activities considered by the young males to be strictly within their provenance. For the next few years Turquoise Trail expeditions were scheduled only intermittently.

In the fall of 1934, a ranch in the Zuni mountains in

northwest New Mexico—440 acres of piñon pines, juniper cedars and high pastures—was purchased by the Howies to use as a base camp. Among its other natural features was a cold, clear stream that flowed through a grove of cottonwood trees. "Cottonwood Gulch" Howie christened the property, and a nonprofit, educational foundation was established to hold title to the land.

A few years later, six small, square, permanent cabins with sides of wany-edged pine were built as sleeping quarters at the base camp. The cabins were designed by Kurt Vonnegut, whose architectural business had hit a disastrous slump during the Depression. His fee: tuition for his 14-year-old son, Kurt Vonnegut, Jr., on the 1937 Trek. Because of his father's long-time connection with the museum, young Vonnegut had participated in other museum-connected activities. As a school representative to the museum's junior board, Kurt Jr. would jump on his bike and pedal down to Saturday morning meetings at the museum. He attended dutifully, though the board, as he would report later at home, seemed rather incomprehensibly preoccupied with birds instead of with general museum operations. No wonder: he had, it was discovered, been slipping into meetings of the bird club instead of the junior board.

Vonnegut, of course, was not the only offspring of museum board members to participate in Prairie Treks. Several other "juniors" as well as grandchildren of board members were among those who, through the years, rattled west in station wagons to visit deserted mining villages, extinct volcanoes and Indian pueblos.

Howie, who had gone back on the Children's Museum board in 1931, was elected first vice president in 1933, a position he held through 1937. After serving as Orchard School headmaster for five years, he resigned in 1938 to go to Yale for a graduate degree, and by the summer of 1938, only about half of the boys on the Prairie Trek roster were from Indianapolis. The city and the Children's Museum were still used as a point of departure, however, until World War II temporarily halted the treks after 1942 and took many of the early trekkers off to wartime camping experiences far removed from House Rock Valley and Sherd Spring Ruin.

CHAPTER SEVEN
The First Lady Comes to Call

Company was coming. Not just your ordinary, giggling, pushing school children. Not even a dignified, respected, Ph.D.-bearing director of another museum. Better than that. The first lady herself, Eleanor Roosevelt, was coming to call at 1150 North Meridian.

Inside the museum, it was controlled bedlam as everything was cleaned, polished and dusted for the visit, which the museum had learned about less than twelve hours earlier. Glass cases sparkled, temporarily rid of the fingerprint smudges of small visitors. Special care had been taken with the arrangement of dozens of dolls clad in authentic, ethnic costumes, and a collection of colorfully embroidered, Brittany-style lace caps with delicate, long streamers. For it was these items, in fact, which were the lure bringing Mrs. Roosevelt to the museum this hot August Friday in 1937. They were the handiwork of some of the Work Projects Administration workers who had been assigned to the museum beginning the previous summer. With WPA being among the cherished arrows in President Roosevelt's quiver of Depression fighters, it made good political sense for his wife to use the small wedge of free time on her crowded day's schedule to visit an institution that would give the program good publicity. After addressing a convention of Young Democrats at Cadle Tabernacle, she was to head for the Children's Museum.

With everything almost ready and nearly an hour left before the time of Mrs. Roosevelt's arrival, a weary Grace Golden cast an eye about for a place where she could lie down for a quick, recuperative rest before the big event. The fastest, easiest thing to do, she decided, was to lay out some news-papers on the floor and stretch out at the rear of the museum's long hall. And there she lay when, shortly thereafter, Mrs. Roosevelt and party walked in the back door—a good forty minutes early.

Despite this unnerving beginning, the official visit was a big success. Mrs. Roosevelt admired the caps, examined the dolls, enthused over the meticulous, small dioramas skillfully constructed by a WPA artist, a white-haired gentleman with a name almost too stirringly American to be true: John Quincy Adams. Escorted by a proud Carr and Mrs. Golden, the first lady, with several state and regional WPA officials in tow, stayed for nearly an hour and insisted on seeing all three floors of the museum.

A month later she gave the museum a brief mention in her daily newspaper column: "I have given the two dolls which were sent me by the Children's Museum in Indianapolis to the library here in the village of Hyde Park, where they are holding an exhibition of dolls. I was delighted to see how appreciative everybody was of the beautiful way in which these dolls are made and dressed. I wish so much that other museums might have the advantage of a painter like John Quincy Adams. . . . He has a great gift for painting backgrounds. I imagine his paintings bring out the various exhibits and attract children more than any other single thing I saw in the museum."

From the beginning, the WPA had proved to be a real boon to the museum. One of these new staff members was Harry Bell, a skilled taxidermist, who later supervised many of the other WPA workers. At last, there were plenty of hands to build cases, help mount exhibits, do repairs and handle the other, innumerable tasks always needing to be done around the old house. The long, oak dining table, which once fed social and political leaders, was now stacked high with pieces of colorful material. All day long from the dining room came the soft voices—many of them with foreign accents—of women chattering as they stitched the fabric into doll costumes. Yet sometimes the happy sounds masked personal, Depression-spawned tragedy. One woman, who hummed all the time as she worked, was asked why by a museum staff member. "If I didn't, I'd cry," she replied simply.

The early part of the decade had been rough on the museum, just as it had been on the country as a whole. Director Carr (he had begun using this title instead of curator early in 1932) postponed taking his salary from time to time, just as he had during his first years with the museum. Sometimes he even advanced the general fund operating money. All members of the small staff were asked to take a month's vacation without pay during the summer of 1934 (which saved $425), and at other times trustees Ben Hitz, Herman Wolff, Fred Bates Johnson and Mrs. Carey would personally pledge to pay staff members' salaries for a number of weeks.

Sadly, some of the stalwart trustees who had kept the museum afloat during its early years were now in danger of sinking themselves. Dwight Ritter, for instance, the board's first treasurer who had personally paid all of the museum's bills during one, early, touch-and-go summer, had to resign from the board in 1934 because of the deteriorating condition of his own business.

An earlier blow had come when the Board of School Commissioners announced that the museum would no longer be allowed to hold inter-school competitions for the greatest percentage of members (such as for the Sousa Cup) or give out the sea horse membership buttons. Even with annual memberships of only twenty-five cents per child, schools in impoverished neighborhoods were placed at too great a disadvantage, claimed some school principals. Without the incentive of competition and buttons the museum's income from pupil and teacher memberships dropped significantly—from $1,779.50 in 1930 to $396.25 in 1932.

Fortunately, school funds did soon come in through another door. Upon learning that the annual $10,000 school board appropriation to the art institute had been obtained through state legislation, the Children's Museum set up its own committee to ask the Indiana General Assembly for something similar. House Bill H185 was passed on March 2, 1931; it permitted the Board of School Commissioners to make appropriations of up to $5,000 annually to the Children's Museum and to appoint one member to the museum board of trustees. At the end of 1931, the museum was told it would receive $2,500 annually (the schools were under economic pressure, too). The museum also had good fortune in the first school board representative appointed, Julian Wetzel, who was soon to become president of the school board and who developed a keen interest in the Children's Museum.

In late 1936, the museum was told it would begin receiving the entire $5,000 appropriation from the school board—after the museum pointed out that it was, in fact, supplying the schools with more than $6,000 worth of services annually. Among those services were the cases full of exhibit material circulated throughout the schools from the museum's lending department, with the school's trucks handling the delivery of cases from museum to school.

The lending department had started humbly enough. Grace Golden had clipped pictures and articles from old *National Geographic* magazines and mounted them on cardboard for teachers to use as extra classroom resource material. "The building of 'miniature museums' (traveling exhibits) to be sent to schools and organizations upon requisition, is a service deserving earnest consideration," Carr told the board in his 1930 annual report. "Frequent calls for special exhibit material have resulted in the sending out of many groups of objects from the permanent collection now containing many duplicates." Mrs. Golden discovered that, during this period, transportation to the museum was a real problem. She felt, as she explained later, that "portable exhibits would bring some beauty into the lives of school children who had only the fog of Depression surrounding them."

By the fall of 1932, the museum, "following the modern trend of museums in larger cities," as it explained in a bulletin to its members, was inaugurating a school extension service. The material from *National Geographic* and other sources had been assembled into packets classified by subject matter. Fifty portable cases, which contained collections of everything from sponges and seaweed to a miniature Navajo loom with half-finished blanket, had been prepared. A neighbor of Mrs. Golden's, a young woman named Estelle Preston who had been forced by financial pressures to drop out of college, had been hired to organize the cases and keep the records that such an operation entailed. (As it turned out, the museum affected her life in many ways; she later married Harry Bell.) Teachers responded with enthusiasm to the portable exhibits as a source of free, creative teaching aids. By 1938, the museum's bulletin could proudly point out that "our turnover in this department is larger and more adequate, compared to our school popu- lation, than that of Chicago, and that city has a foundation of more than a million dollars for that specific purpose."

The Indianapolis museum might not have a million-dollar foundation, but it did have shrewd trustees. One day in the mid-1930s, board members Herman Wolff and Fred Bates Johnson invited Mrs. Robert Failey to have lunch with them at Ayres' popular eighth-floor Tea Room. Mrs. Failey was inter- ested in the museum and had recently been chairman of its education committee. But now the two men had another project for her. Would she, they wanted to know, be willing to see if she could talk her friend Ruth Lilly into accepting a position on the museum board? Mrs. Failey's husband and Eli Lilly (grandson and namesake of the pharmaceutical company founder) had been chums since boyhood, and after Lilly's mar- riage to Ruth Allison, Mrs. Failey and the new Mrs. Lilly also had become good friends. Mrs. Failey's sales job was appar- ently a good one; Ruth Allison Lilly began her first term as a trustee in 1935. (Though the first Mrs. Lilly, Evelyn Fortune, had been appointed to the board in 1927, she had never been very active and had served only briefly.) Such was not to be the case with Ruth Lilly, who gave much time and attention to the affairs of the museum and, in 1938, became a vice president of the board.

Wolff had come up with another particularly good idea earlier in the decade. What the museum needed, he pointed out at a board meeting in September 1933, was a "junior aux- iliary" of young women college graduates. Some years earlier, there had been, very briefly, another Children's Museum Guild. An already-existing women's club had approached the board in late 1927 about changing its name and taking on the museum as its project. It was understood by the museum

board that the group's function was to be primarily fund raising; instead, its activities turned out to be chiefly social. Less
than a year later, in 1928, the museum board, concerned that
there would be confusion between membership drives sponsored by the museum itself and the group using the name
Children's Museum Guild, asked the group to give up the
museum name.

The arrangement with the new group turned out to be
much more successful. A few suitable young ladies were contacted, and by December 1933, these new volunteers were
helping with office work. "The museum," said Mr. Carr, is
"greatly indebted." Each volunteer would spend one morning
at the museum every two weeks, sometimes even doing research or guiding tours of children. They also assisted with
membership calls. By the spring of 1934 help was being supplied by eight young ladies—Mrs. Robert W. Todd, Mrs.
Thomas Sinclair and Misses Anne Ayres, Julianne Campbell,
Joanne Dissette, Martha Slaymaker, Melissa Wadley and Ruth
Zinn. More official praise was tendered to the volunteers when
Miss Dissette, chairman of the informal group, attended the
museum board's March 1934 luncheon meeting, as usual at the
small, elegant Glenn-Martin Hotel, where the food was good
and the location (946 North Meridian) handy to the museum.

Mrs. Frank Sisson, the daughter of a friend of Grace
Golden's, soon became involved in activities of the new guild,
and was elected first president as the small group became more
formally organized with dues and regular meetings. In 1934 an
Irvington branch of the guild was begun, and by 1936, each
group had an active membership of twelve. The women assisted with some of the new fund-raising ideas that were being
tried by the museum, including an event which turned out to
be the most successful in providing funds and publicity—a
large, annual, glass and china show at L.S. Ayres department
store. Guild members also began a speakers' bureau to help
Mrs. Golden continue spreading the word about the museum
in the community.

Though these extra workers supplied welcome assistance,
the museum still had pressing needs in many areas. Luckily,
Arthur Carr was a scrounger. He had the ability to know who

was getting rid of what and how it might be valuable to the museum. He went to auctions. He showed up at demolition sites to snag items that had historical significance or, if not that, at least some years of use left in them. "He follows the house-wreckers around town . . ." was the way *Indianapolis Times* columnist Anton Scherrer put it in one of his popular "Our Town" columns. "Mr. Carr found Henry Ward Beecher's front door that way; his mantelpiece, too. That was years ago, of course, when the house-wreckers pounced on Mr. Beecher's old home—the one that used to be on the south side of Ohio St. opposite the entrance of Cadle Tabernacle. It was the place, too, where Mr. Beecher raised the first cauliflower grown in Indianapolis. Mr. Carr says he hung around the Beecher place until the house-wreckers gave him what he wanted—just to get rid of him.

"Well, you ought to see what Mr. Carr has done with the Beecher relics," Scherrer continued. "He's fixed up a period room (circa 1860) on the third floor of the Children's Museum, and to get into it you have to go through the old Beecher doorway. It's the slickest approach since the Herron Art people thought of putting a horse in front of their place."

Among the things Carr had acquired somewhere were fifty-two cherry cases which lined the walls and formed two back-to-back rows down the middle of what, in earlier days, had been the front, second-floor bedroom. Now the room was the nature room, and the eye-level (for middle-sized boys and girls) cases were filled with mounted birds arranged in carefully re-created settings. Heads hung all over the walls, and on top of the cases were larger, mounted animals—squirrels, a small boa constrictor and, the great favorite of all the children, a large, embalmed monkey (which was probably really a baboon). It looked a bit wrinkled and dried (not surprisingly), and its tail curled around the branch on which it had been posed for posterity.

Mrs. Golden hated the monkey as heartily as the children liked it. She felt the same about one of the room's other occupants, a two-headed calf. (The calf was eventually banished to the basement, and one of the storage rooms down there was

The shelter house at Garfield Park was the museum's second home.

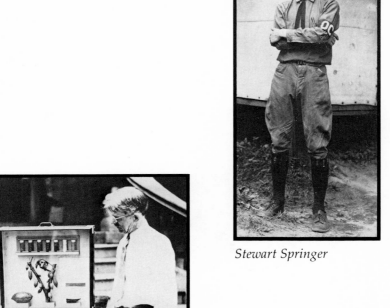

Stewart Springer

Arthur B. Carr

The Carey house at 1150 North Meridian was the museum's third home.
Indianapolis Star photo

The paneled room in the Carey house became the museum's reading room.
Indianapolis Star photo

*Arthur Carr was joined in the operation of
the museum by Grace Golden in 1928.*
W. Frank Jones photo

*Some of the members of the museum's junior board in 1929 were
(front row) Mildred Trueblood, Doris Young, Agnes Coldwell, Rachel
Cartwright, Fred Cimmerman; (back row) Louise Rhodehamel, Virginia
Ruth, Margaret Hedges, Maxine Peters and Mary Ellen Voyles.*

An early poster advertised the new museum to the citizens of Indianapolis.

Prairie Trekkers made casts of dinosaur footprints in the Painted Desert.

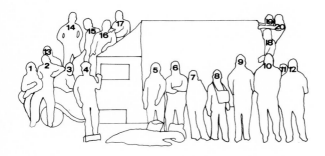

Members of the 1930 Prairie Trek expedition, posing in the museum's front yard before departure, were: (1) Arthur Schultz, (2) Ben Rubush, (3) Gene Iglehart, (4) Bill Herron, (5) Charles Latham, (6) John Ragsdale, (7) Eddie Craft, (8) Alan Appel, (9) leader Hillis Howie, (10) counselor Gordon Thompson, (11) Dan Taylor, (12) counselor Herb Sweet, (13) Edward Tice, (14) Jack Kittle, (15) Robert Hamilton, (16) Arthur Crane, (17) Paull Torrence, (18) Lefferts Hutton, (19) Arthur Zinkin, (20) Jim Failey.

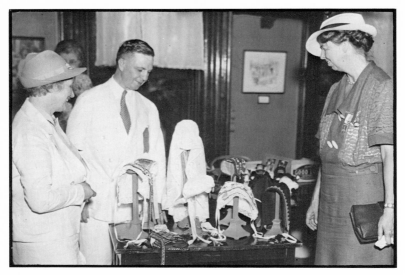

First lady Eleanor Roosevelt (right) came to see WPA projects at the museum during a 1937 visit to Indianapolis. With her were Ruth Neibert, supervisor of the women's and professional division of WPA, and John K. Jennings, WPA state administrator.
Indianapolis Times photo

Grace Golden (left) looks at costumed dolls being made at the museum by WPA workers.

Members of the museum's Bird Lover's Club prepare a Christmas feast for the birds in the late 1930s.

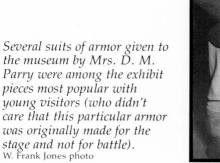

Several suits of armor given to the museum by Mrs. D. M. Parry were among the exhibit pieces most popular with young visitors (who didn't care that this particular armor was originally made for the stage and not for battle).
W. Frank Jones photo

Doll exhibits were held often at the museum during its early years.

An upstairs hall of the Carey house had become the European gallery by the late 1930s. W. Frank Jones photo

called, from then on, "the calf room.") The children loved the nature room not only because of its fascinating, creepy animal specimens but because this was the room with the secret compartment, a sliding panel in the fireplace mantel which evidently was where the house's earlier occupants had hidden valuables.

It was against Carr's nature to refuse anything, whether it was the Borden collection, part of which was acquired in 1934, or an embalmed monkey, two-headed calf or another sewing machine. Mrs. Golden claimed he had fifty sewing machines stashed up under the attic's eaves, which was where he also stored many old phonographs. As more and more things arrived, some of the building's display areas began, in effect, to turn into storage areas. Yet many of what Carr considered his true "treasures" were kept hidden away and pulled out only for special visitors. Part of this was Carr's concern, a legitimate one, about theft. Despite Carr's standing instructions to Mrs. Golden, Estelle Preston, Harry Bell and others to "watch the floors" (i.e. keep a sharp eye on visitors), things disappeared. Often, missing items would be found in the restrooms of the filling station next door to the museum.

Yet this wasn't the only reason that Carr hid away some items. He was just plain secretive and acquisitive, a collector. He was evidently not an unfamiliar type among museum professionals. One day when Carr was away from the museum, a woman from out of town who was associated with another museum stopped by to visit. Miss Preston gave her a tour of the facility, and finally, just before she left, the visitor said, "I can just picture what your director is like. He just loves to hide things and he'll let only very special people see his real treasures." She had it just about right, Miss Preston had to admit.

Carr also was ambivalent about his main customers—the children. Because he and Mrs. Carr had no children, he never had to develop a tolerance at home for the noise and dirty fingerprints that are as inevitable with children as freckles and toothless grins. (The fleas that go with the dog, so to speak.) Smudged hand prints all over the display cases distressed him. However, he could be patient and tolerant as he let youngsters handle Eskimo spear points and Indian arrowheads and showed them the difference between good workmanship and bad.

Carr was an indefatigable worker, spending long hours at the museum and missing meals, much to the distress of his quiet, soft-spoken wife who worried constantly about his health (for good reason—he did usually come down with pneumonia every winter). Agile and quick-moving, Carr rushed about constantly all day to get as much as possible accomplished for the museum. He and the museum's custodian took care of most of the building's maintenance themselves. Carr, though now in his sixties, was absolutely fearless about climbing up and around anything—the high roof of the old house to clean out gutters; the second-floor front stairway railing to nail up special exhibit hangings; the small branches of the high maple trees in the front yard to hang the American flag before a presidential caravan (Hoover, this time) streamed past down Meridian.

The extreme frugality with which Carr operated the museum meant that even paint was bought, if not second-hand, at least on sale. He would regularly go to a nearby hardware store and buy a gallon of this and a gallon of that—whatever was being closed out, regardless of color. Back at the museum, all were dumped together and all rooms needing painting were, for a time, this unique, impossible-to-duplicate shade— usually something between a mustard and a beige.

Like classic cars and women of what Europeans tactfully call "a certain age," older houses need increasing amounts of preventive maintenance if they are to retain their charm. But maintenance requires money, and the 60-year-old Carey house was beginning to show the effects of the museum's years of not having any. Two furnaces with gargantuan appetites for coal sat facing each other in the basement of the old house; they produced about as much trouble as heat. Clouds of dark smoke sometimes would roll out through the registers, and during one particularly cold winter, the pipes froze, as did the water in the fish tanks. Staff members, who had been wearing coats while they worked, finally gave up and closed the museum for two months, taking work home to do.

Plaster fell from the ceiling in the auditorium and the electrical wiring was also showing signs of age. No more than ten children at a time could be allowed up in the third-floor galleries because the stairway was narrow and winding and there was no fire escape. A cistern in the back of the house overflowed into the basement after every rain, making the exhibit material stored down there moldy and the upper floors damp. Not ideal surroundings for either man or fossil.

Though interim repairs were made (Mrs. Carey had apparently agreed to take care of the bills), the board decided its housing committee needed to look seriously for a new location. Other large buildings and old houses were studied, but nothing looked hopeful. Then late in 1936, William Rockwood, vice president and treasurer of a prosperous, old, local manufacturing company and member of the museum board for three years, made a dazzling announcement. He and his wife had moved from their home at Thirty-sixth and Washington Boulevard out to Spring Mill Road. The Washington Boulevard house had been sold, but the 200-foot-by-280-foot lot next door was not. That, the Rockwoods were giving to the museum, it was announced at the November board meeting. The news was greeted by a standing vote of thanks from the other trustees.

Architect Vonnegut was ready with plans at the next board meeting. The two-story, clean-lined, modernistic building would have lots of glass brick to provide natural light for exhibit cases. There would be four galleries, an auditorium seating 240 and a separate rear entrance for school buses. Tentative cost for the first unit of the new building was estimated at $76,000 (thirty cents per cubic foot). WPA funds would, it was hoped, be available for some aspects of construction costs. Mr. and Mrs. Eli Lilly offered to donate $25,000 for the new building (there had been some discussion earlier about Lilly giving the Children's Museum his Indiana historical collection as well as some funds to help provide appropriate fireproof housing). Another standing vote of thanks from the trustees.

But then a zoning hearing in May 1937 burst the bubble. The museum would ruin the neighborhood, claimed residents of the area, depreciating property values as much as "25 to 35 percent." By a vote of seven to two, the city plan commission decided not to grant the museum's petition for a zoning variance. Museum supporters were devastated. Still, the museum did now have the Rockwood lot, which would be useful in the future to trade for other property or sell.

Not only was the Carey house in need of repairs, but it also was still, technically, a temporary location, and efforts to pin down a specific time commitment from Mrs. Carey had, in the past, been a bit tricky. Mrs. Carey, who loved giving others gifts, could sometimes be almost impetuously generous, said family observers. On these occasions, the younger, hard-headed businessmen in the family often would step in to discourage what they considered excessive largesse. Back in 1929, for instance, Vonnegut, then board president, had excitedly reported to the other trustees a telephone conversation in which Mrs. Carey had said the museum could stay in the house for at least five years. At the board meeting two months later, however, Mrs. Carey asked to have the statement about the telephone conversation "clarified" to show that, should the opportunity to sell or rent the property at 1150 North Meridian present itself, she would be free "to make such arrangements." The board dutifully responded that it was "grateful for the present opportunity, but would not wish to hamper any such action by the owner of the property." In June 1934, she again told the board she was willing to give a written agreement that the museum could occupy the house for ten years unless some offer of a very unusual nature presented itself. Mrs. Carey's statement added that she regretted that the present status of her estate precluded her from giving the building to the trustees.

Though she was still a board member, Mrs. Carey had withdrawn a bit more into the background of museum operations as the years passed and other, distracting, personal sadness intervened. (A second daughter, Mary June Appel, had died in the early '30s after a long illness.) She generally channeled her ideas and wishes through board members Fred Bates Johnson, her lawyer, and Mrs. Donald Jameson, whose mother-in-law, Mrs. Ovid Butler Jameson, was her first cousin.

The advancing years, however, had not diminished her love of travel or her sense of fun. On a 1937 North Cape cruise with two grandsons, she gamely dressed as a brown-robed monk for the ship's costume party—and won first prize. After this, she embarked on a trip across Russia. But this exotic journey was to be her last. She was taken ill, returned to Indianapolis and died at Methodist Hospital on June 14, 1938, at age 79. Two days later, a funeral service was held in the late afternoon at Haverway Farm. "Through trials and heartaches, through bitter loss and desolation she kept her poise and smiled her way and won her victory and made the sunshine in her world," said the minister at the services.

The obituaries were lengthy, the tributes effusive. "A woman of remarkable attainments," said an editorial in the *Indianapolis News*. "Her interests were so varied and distinguished that it would be difficult to class them according to their importance. However, it is probable that she was most widely known for her singularly successful work as the founder and chief patron of the Children's Museum. . . . It will forever remain a tribute to her interest in children. . . . She was ever-alert to the development of the moment, yet she never wavered in her fidelity to basic truths and the wisdom that comes of living well in the light of the past." Said a resolution of tribute adopted by the Children's Museum's board: "Research into Mrs. Carey's interests proves her love for the things that carry the best of the past into a useful combination with the modern. Thus the museum is a manifestation of her spirit. The children of Indianapolis have lost a good and loving friend. The directors and staff of the museum have lost a patron and leader whose place can never be filled."

Of the five who had gotten together fourteen years earlier in the winter of 1924 to discuss starting a museum for children, now only Faye Henley was left on the board. Miss Browning had died in 1927; Miss Fitch, in 1937. Murray Dalman, who had returned to Indianapolis in 1932 to become principal of several Indianapolis grade schools, never again was very active in museum affairs, though he was named chairman of a science subcommittee in the mid-1930s. And from among the museum's original nine trustees, only Miss Henley and Vonnegut remained on the board.

In Mrs. Carey's will, filed for probate a week after her death, Wheeler City Rescue Mission received $1,000, Orchard School and Christamore House each received $2,000, John Herron Art Institute received funds to complete a $5,000 sub-scription made earlier and the Children's Museum received $5,000. Yet her true bequest to the Children's Museum was more than funds. She had, simply, begun it all.

CHAPTER EIGHT
New Hand at the Helm

Grace Golden. What a gloriously euphonious name. No Hollywood agent could have come up with a name any more appropriate for the role in life that Grace Blaisdell would someday play. The name had not only alliteration, but a misty aura of quality, of status, of affluence—things that were to mean a great deal to Grace Blaisdell Golden.

By the late 1930s, it had become apparent, both to those who loved her and those who found her abrasive, that Grace Golden was extremely talented. She was a handsome woman, tall and stately, with short, dark hair worn in marcelled waves close to the side of her head in the style of the day. She was to some a "near genius" in her ability to generate publicity for the museum, to give exciting, inspiring speeches and to charm useful people in the community into becoming involved in museum affairs. The annual glass and china show and the Children's Museum Guild blossomed under her direction. And she seemed to have a genuine vision of the educational potential of a children's museum.

In addition to publicity writing, she began branching out into writings of other kinds. She tried her hand at magazine articles, and she wrote a slim children's book, *Pueblo People,* which was published in 1935 by Folkway Press of Indianapolis. She had a writer's eye for detail and the telling anecdote—often museum-supplied. She once wrote about a little red-haired boy who had tagged along with a regular touring school group, watching and listening carefully as Mrs. Golden pointed out various examples of Chinese handiwork: jade and mother-of-pearl ornaments, tiny porcelain figurines, a delicate, carved ivory button. He heard her describe the Chinese as fine craftsmen and lovers of beauty, and after the school group had left, he approached her timidly.

"Lady, I want to tell you something that my mother told me never to tell anybody in the whole world," he said. "My grandfather was an Irish sailor. Once when he sailed to China he married a Chinese woman and took her back to Ireland. So you see, my own grandmother was Chinese. My mother has always been ashamed of it and told me not to speak of her. When you told us of the fine things the Chinese make I was proud of my grandmother for the first time in my life. I wanted you to know." And then the boy disappeared, wrote Mrs. Golden, before she could swallow the lump in her throat.

Not only did Mrs. Golden have obvious flair and imagination, but she was developing true expertise in a number of fields—glass and antiques, for instance. In 1938 she began writing a weekly newspaper column, "Know Your Heirlooms," in the *Indianapolis Star,* and she later taught a class on the same subject at Butler University. Her knowledge of the museum profession and techniques also was continually expanding. In 1937 the American Association of Museums formed a children's museum division and both Carr and Mrs. Golden became involved in its activities. A year later, because of her success in supervising WPA workers at the Children's Museum, Mrs. Golden was appointed field supervisor of the WPA Statewide Museum Project sponsored by the Indiana Historical Society. For several months she visited WPA workers at small museums around the state, instructing them on many aspects of museum operations—cataloging, exhibit design, installation and public relations.

All of this, of course, was increasing her visibility within the museum field. But the real professional plum came later in 1938. With help from Carr, Mrs. Golden was selected as one of twenty-one museum staff members from throughout the United States (and the only one from a children's museum) to

receive a Carnegie Foundation grant to travel and study overseas. For two months she traveled through Poland, Hungary,
Czechoslovakia, Yugoslavia and Holland, studying costumes,
customs and folklore, meeting national leaders and even addressing the International Congress of Press Women in Budapest. No wonder she wrote in notes for a speech sometime
later, "Never been the same since."

Ten years from part-time fund raiser to speaker at an
international conference, if not overnight success, was nonetheless impressive career progress. What made it even more
remarkable was that, for Grace Golden, this had been a by-her-
own-bootstraps operation. For several reasons her early formal
education had been spotty. Born in June 1899, young Grace
had reached her full height at a very early age. Perhaps partially because of this rapid growth, her childhood had been
marked by periods of "sickly" health which kept her out of
school.

The Blaisdells lived and worked (Charles Blaisdell owned
a grocery) on Indianapolis' west side, where Grace's grand-
parents earlier had founded the Wesley Methodist Church.
Several years later, after the flooding White River devastated
much of west-side Indianapolis, her family moved to Twelfth
and Broadway. Even if poor health kept their daughter out of
the regular classroom much of the time, Grace's parents saw to
it that their daughter was educated in other ways. Her father,
of whom she was very fond, would take his little daughter into
a room, hold her up in his arms and tell her to look carefully
all around. Once they were outside he would have her repeat
to him everything she had seen. This was the reason, she
explained in later years, for her unusually good powers of
observation. Her mother, too, was determined that her daughter would be exposed to the things she considered important.
They went to concerts, to lectures, to exhibits. And if there had
been a children's museum in Indianapolis when Grace had
been growing up, she undoubtedly would have been taken
there, too.

In 1918, when Grace Blaisdell was 18, she became assistant secretary of the Indiana Association for the Study and

Prevention of Tuberculosis, having been earlier a part-time worker for the association. Two years later she was named the association's educational secretary. Through friends at Fort Harrison, she was introduced to a man named Byon Maxwell Golden. Max Golden was hearty and good-humored, an excellent salesman who represented a company that made X-ray equipment. In 1921, they were married in a ceremony in her parents' home, and two years later, a baby daughter, Nanci, was born. From Woodruff Place the young family moved, in the late 1920s, to an apartment at 2100 East Michigan, and when Max and Grace Golden separated (they were finally divorced in 1933), Mrs. Golden and her little daughter for a time rented the front room in the apartment of the Preston family across the hall.

Her hiring by the Children's Museum in 1928 was, as it turned out, to have a profound effect on both the museum and Mrs. Golden. She had learned about fund raising and public relations in work she had done for the TB association and the Near East Relief Society. And now she would learn about museums. She listened and watched and absorbed. Not only was she a voracious reader, but she was ambitious and determined to educate herself. She took courses and later talked Estelle Preston into enrolling with her in Indiana University extension classes. And sometimes when it looked as if the evening's class might be interesting to Nanci (movies, for instance, as part of a unit on visual education), the little girl got to go along—always great fun, for there was hot chocolate afterwards.

Mrs. Golden made sure her young daughter was receiving a good education by enrolling her in a parochial school just a block from the museum. The proximity of mama and the museum proved to be more temptation than little Nanci could resist, however. When Nanci was excused from catechism class, she was supposed to report to the school's music teacher. Instead, the little girl would skip down the street to the museum, climb up on a workbench in the basement and watch all the exciting projects that Enie, the carpenter, and George, the janitor were working on. When Mrs. Golden looked out the window and saw a nun, black habit billowing out behind, hurrying down Meridian Street toward the museum, she knew that Nanci had run away—again.

Although Arthur Carr, given his nature, might have preferred running everything himself, he realized that the museum needed what Grace Golden had to offer, if it were to survive and prosper. But their personalities and their abilities were very different. He was quiet, kindly, serious. She was effervescent, an excellent public speaker. She could be warm and generous—or devastatingly sharp-tongued. In one thing, however, they were absolutely alike: they were devoted to the museum. In the early years they worked well together, but later their disagreements and sometimes-loud arguments became more frequent. So frequent and loud, in fact, that the board occasionally dispatched president Margaret Jameson to quiet things down in the back part of the first floor where both of their offices were (his, a small, windowless room; hers, a larger room with many windows).

Much of the time Carr did the museum cataloging at his home, in a small, first-floor room just off the parlor. This practice Mrs. Golden found frustrating, for many of the records were not where she could get to them. Their attitude about how museum pieces should be used also differed. To him they should be taken care of, cherished, maybe even tucked away. To her they were there to be used—for promotion, to educate children.

In 1942, Arthur Carr turned 70. His health had not been good, and during his absence because of illness, Mrs. Golden had assumed more and more of the museum's leadership responsibilities. With her travels she was becoming better-known within the museum profession and in Indianapolis. Now her eye was definitely on the directorship of the Children's Museum. But it was difficult for Carr to leave. He loved the museum he had served since 1926 and, as staff members said, would have happily stayed there until he was 100. Actually, since the late 1930s, the board had been trying to get across to Carr that the time of his directorship was drawing to an end. Part of the problem, they felt, was that he did not always see the museum as a place to be used by children. Said one of the board's recommendations for the future of the museum, "The staff should stay alert to new movements in the museum field," and make sure that the museum was "for children in spirit as well as in name."

In January 1941, Faye Henley proposed at a board meeting that an administrative committee be formed to consult weekly with the staff, try to codify specific responsibilities of various staff members and lighten Carr's load (at his concerned wife's request) to primarily curatorial duties. Not that delegations of responsibility on paper made much difference—Carr continued to do pretty much what he had been doing.

For museum board and staff members, already concerned, like the rest of the country, over the wartime events in Europe and the Pacific, there was added the distress of divided loyalties on the question of the museum directorship. Many were fond of Carr, yet they felt he was not the person to lead the museum into the new decade. (But easing him out was a little like "trying to chop the head off a turtle," as one board member put it.) Some trustees felt that Mrs. Golden could provide energetic and dynamic leadership. Others—board president Fred Bates Johnson, for instance—felt that even when Carr did retire, his job should not go to Mrs. Golden.

Bates Johnson (he was usually called by his middle name) was officially named to the board of trustees in 1932. However, he had been involved in museum affairs since the very beginning, for he was the lawyer whom the museum organizers had consulted about the constitution and bylaws. He was a short, feisty man with a lot of ideas, given to speaking his mind in no uncertain terms—"a delightful frankness," his friends sometimes called it.

In March 1942, Mrs. Golden went to see Johnson in his law office. After discussing general museum affairs, Johnson, according to a letter Mrs. Golden wrote a month later, "said that his friendly advice to me was that I seek a better paying position in one of the war efforts and named a particular job which he said he would help me procure if I wanted him to." Mrs. Golden demurred, saying that she intended to stay in the museum field "which paid in satisfactions what it lacked in salary." Besides, she said, "certain trustees" had led her to assume that she would be the next director. Johnson replied that although he, personally, would not recommend her for the post, he would convene a group of any six trustees she chose to hear her plans for the future of the institution and her reasons for feeling that she should have the directorship.

Part of Johnson's objections apparently had something to do with the way Mrs. Golden had handled some of the WPA workers. He also felt, some thought, that the job should go to a man. Evidently other trustees also objected to what they saw as her pushing Carr out of the job—and none too gently. At the April board meeting, Carr's resignation as director effective June 1, 1942, was read. He was, however, to continue working part-time to finish organizing curatorial records and storage facilities. Johnson, said Mrs. Golden, did not, as he had promised, convene the six trustees before her status was determined. Instead, at a special meeting at Johnson's home, it had been decided that she would be acting head of the museum, "while the Board of Trustees endeavor to secure a permanent Director." With that, Mrs. Golden gave the board her resignation. "Unlike Mr. Carr, . . . I shall not be on call," she added emphatically. In another letter she explained her actions: "I determined that if my long employment had not served as a long enough probationary period, there would be no term of acting directorship for me."

The board was thrown into a tizzy. Sometime earlier Estelle Bell had also submitted her resignation (though she continued to work part-time); the museum would be without its three mainstays. Interestingly enough, Carr had unofficially conveyed to the board his strong feelings that Mrs. Golden should be his successor. A special board meeting of the fifteen trustees (the board had been expanded in 1927) was called for May 18, 1942, at Johnson's Fletcher Trust Building law office. With Johnson absent from the room, board vice president Reily Adams presided. By a unanimous vote of the nine trustees present, Grace Golden was named the new director of the Children's Museum. Johnson's one-sentence letter of resignation as board president (dated fourteen days earlier) was immediately tendered and accepted, though he stayed on the board and would, in future years, frequently head important committees.

Carr was given the title of director emeritus, and a luncheon was held in his honor at the Indianapolis Athletic Club on the first Monday in June, 1942. He was presented a parchment scroll as the second member of the Order of the Golden Sea Horse, a ceremonial honor devised two years earlier to honor Faye Henley on the fifteenth anniversary of the museum. "I am sincerely grateful for the rare privilege of service," said Carr in a statement he read at the luncheon. Gracefully, he toasted the board's past presidents, its new president, Mrs. Norman Baxter, and its new director, "Mrs. Grace Golden, my efficient associate worker through nearly fourteen years. . . . To her has been tossed the torch with which she will lead our beloved institution. . . ."

With that concluded, all concerned took a deep breath and turned their full attention to the effects World War II was having on operations at 1150 North Meridian.

CHAPTER NINE
Keep 'em Flying, Keep 'em Chirping

Given the events of December 7, 1941, it was not surprising that the Children's Museum had decided to put its Japanese exhibits in storage. The popular Japanese Room, with its jinriksha and life-size jinriksha man, its beautiful kimono-clad doll from the International Children's Society of Japan, had first opened in a main floor room with bay window back in 1932. Later, a few pieces from other Far Eastern countries were added, and its name was changed to the Oriental Room. The preponderance of material was Japanese, however, which meant there was now quite a gap in the Oriental Room exhibits. It was to be filled by borrowed material on India and China, two countries suddenly more appropriate for attention from America's children.

The museum—all museums—had defined for themselves a specific role to play in the drama of the country at war. The Association of Museum Directors pledged that American museums would be "sources of inspiration illuminating the past and vivifying the present; . . . they will fortify the spirit on which Victory depends." In Indianapolis, the Children's Museum's quarterly bulletin, published two months after war was declared, quoted remarks from a similar publication put out by the Illinois State Museum. "Now when America is confronted with the forces of militarism which are striking at modern civilization, our first thought is to support our armed forces; our second thoughts must be to preserve our priceless culture. . . . In a troubled and oftentimes dishonest world . . . the museum extends a calm and soothing hand and shows us that our culture lives on."

Again, lest anyone think museums were expendable in time of crisis, the same point was made in a museum membership campaign letter sent to all Indianapolis school teachers a month later. "When the smoke of war has cleared away, there still will be children who must carry on our precious American heritage. To this end, in spite of our trying times, American culture must be preserved and interpreted." (The letter raised $820 in teacher memberships.)

As with everyone else in the country, even the museum's constituents, the children, were helping with the war effort. At home they peeled labels off cans and stamped them flat to save tin. They took containers of accumulated drippings from the breakfast bacon to school for "fat drives" which, they vaguely understood, had something or other to do with making bombs. They saved their dimes and bought victory stamps with pictures of the Lexington Minuteman on them. In school music classes, in addition to singing traditional grade school songs like "Blue Tail Fly" and "Men of Harlech," they now learned "We're the Seabees of the Navy" and "The Caissons Go Rolling Along."

Children pitched in at the museum as well. A few years earlier the guild had begun a series of after-school hobby classes on a variety of subjects ranging from making models of airplanes and clipper ships to nature study. Now many of the hobby clubs were busy with wartime tasks. Around the World Club members made scrapbooks to send to children in bomb shelters in England. The young girls in Needlecrafters knitted six-inch yarn squares which the Red Cross would make into afghans for refugees.

Though wartime gasoline rationing drastically curtailed the numbers of school groups coming to the museum, business did pick up in other ways. Full industrial mobilization meant that many mothers were going to work; others were doing war-connected volunteer work. Children were sometimes left to their own devices, and often they headed for the museum. In some families, the father might be working the night shift and sleeping days. Instead of playing at home, where they were continually "shushed," children came to the museum. Later, a play area with tables and benches and improvised teeter-totter was placed in the museum's back yard for what Mrs. Golden called, in a report to the board, "stray boys in the neighborhood who have no place to play."

But it was not just children at loose ends who were making the hand counter at the museum's reception desk click faster. With gas rationing, there were few out-of-town sight-seeing trips in the car on weekends. Instead, families were doing things together in town. Because of this, the museum began special Family Sundays. At first, special lectures were scheduled on Russian icons, the Philippines, Poland—but it was discovered that it was hard for speakers to hit just the right level for both parents and children. So Family Sundays were reorganized, with individual schools sponsoring a Sunday afternoon at the museum. Students, teachers and parents were all encouraged to visit—in effect school trips without gas-consuming chartered buses. This new approach proved to be extremely successful. During a three-hour period on one May 1944 Sunday afternoon, 1,032 people visited.

Gasoline, of course, was not the only item in short supply. Coal, too, was scarce, and in May 1943, Mrs. Golden was advised by the board to "buy any she could secure" for the following winter. With paper needed for the war effort, not much extra was available for the home front, and the quarterly bulletin was cut back in size. Later in the war, a special city-wide waste-paper drive was organized by the Marion County Salvage Committee, with the Children's Museum to receive the profits. A very respectable $3,450 was turned over to the museum and promptly deposited in the building fund.

Mrs. Golden had discovered that the stresses of wartime (even in sheltered America) tended to shorten children's attention spans and scatter their interests. Therefore, to hold the interest of the children better, as well as to attract more visitors, the museum began a program of rotating exhibits, which, in turn, provided opportunities for more publicity. Many of the exhibits, too, were war-connected. In the winter of 1943, as far away on the Volga, the bitter, five-month siege of Stalingrad came to an end, the museum opened an exhibit of loaned

Russian items (mostly religious pieces). Commented the *Indianapolis Times,* in an article about the exhibit, "Russia's stand against our common foe, Germany, naturally directs our attention to the Russian people. And we wonder about the background of the courageous Russian soldier." The museum held a special evening program to collect items for the Russian war relief; it netted 300 garments, 21 pairs of shoes and 107 bars of soap. Later, the Indianapolis Committee for Aid to Poland (of which Mrs. Golden was chairman) also organized a collection of clothing and sewing supplies. Mrs. Golden, who had brought back from Poland a large number of Polish language books, bundled them up and sent them to Polish refugee settlements in Mexico and other places where Polish-language anything would be hard to come by.

Alaska didn't need war relief. It was, however, a place where Indianapolis fathers and big brothers were stationed, as the museum's bulletin pointed out in an article about the new Eskimo exhibit, which had opened in the redecorated and reorganized Indian and Eskimo gallery. The Eskimo pieces which the museum had acquired were part of a fine collection put together by Dr. and Mrs. Henry W. Greist, medical missionaries for seventeen years at Point Barrow, Alaska. There were examples of Eskimo clothing and hunting and household articles and a cut-away model of a driftwood, sod and snow Eskimo hut, made by pupils at the mission school. There were also rare, prehistoric Eskimo pieces, including flint skin scrapers, a stone axe and bone plugs which were worn through the cheeks as decoration. This was not the first missionary collection the museum had acquired, for Mr. and Mrs. Carr, who were active church members, had contacts in the mission field. As a matter of fact, former missionaries and navy personnel had turned out to be one reason for the growing strength of the ethnic collections in the Children's Museum—and, indeed, other midwestern museums.

Mrs. Golden also used the exhibits about other countries to begin preparing her young visitors for the time after the war when all people in the world would again try to get along together. "Crafts that tell something of the life and customs of a strange people, implements of everyday use in a strange land, all create in children a tolerance for the people whose way of life differs from their own," she wrote in a museum bulletin. She added that long before Wendell Willkie wrote *One World*, "Children's museum workers everywhere were stressing the very things about which we hear so much today—a broader knowledge of the people of other lands and races. . . ."

The war brought other changes as well. Several members of the board of trustees went off to active duty. Contributions, when they were made to the museum, now were often in the form of war bonds. Yet some things stayed the same—feeding the birds at Christmas time, for instance. The museum's exhortation to "Keep 'em Flying," in this instance, meant cardinals and chickadees, not B-17s. The Christmas feast for the birds had grown from a simple Saturday program of Mrs. Donald C. Drake's Bird Lovers Club in 1935, to a full-blown program of winter care for the birds. Three hundred bird shelters were placed on the grounds of Marion County schools, and the governor recommended that the Christmas feast become state-wide.

Mrs. Drake also helped the museum organize a very successful spring vacation gala for children at the World War Memorial to honor the cardinal on the tenth anniversary of its selection as the Indiana state bird. Everyone was given packets of sunflower seeds to take home and plant the next summer to raise food for the birds. "Don't put your feathered friends on ration cards," said the accompanying message. "They will stay with you all winter with a little care. Keep 'em Flying. Keep 'em Chirping."

The end of the WPA-supplied workers, as well as increased defense requirements, meant that the museum, like many other segments of the country, found itself short-handed. Museum stalwart Faye Henley joined the staff to help with the extension department for nearly a year. Guild members pitched in by serving as afternoon gallery guides, though with transportation problems and a longer school day, many after-school activities, such as the hobby clubs, eventually were moved to Saturdays. The guild also developed museum games—paper-and-pencil activities and quizzes—which youngsters could complete by reading labels and otherwise studying the exhibits throughout the museum.

Another paper-and-pencil activity that had long been popular with the children was gallery sketching. Stacked in a closet near the reception desk were canvas camp stools and wooden drawing boards. Children would take a stool and board and pencil and paper and go off to find something interesting to draw. For girls this often turned out to be dolls; for the boys, the marvelously menacing, mounted bear.

Relations between the museum and the schools continued to be good. In the early part of the decade the school board had not only provided the supervision and labor to make roof, chimney and other outside repairs to the museum building, but it also had assigned an experienced teacher to the museum full-time to teach social studies to visiting classes, using the museum study collections. Though later there were some problems with the arrangement when the school system's visual education department got involved, by 1945 the museum board was ready to ask that the teaching service be reestablished. And that was not all the museum asked for. It was time, it said, for the Board of School Commissioners to increase financial support for the museum from $5,000 annually to $8,500. (A bill had just passed the legislature allowing school systems to increase museum appropriations to $15,000 annually.) The school board agreed, and the following December, the museum received $4,250, a payment for the first half of 1946.

In their efforts to provide service to all the children of the city, the museum and the guild were faced with a problem. Indianapolis was still a city with racially segregated schools. When visits to the museum were mainly in family groups or school classes, those two general social units, in effect, took care of who came. (Classes from Negro schools—the term "black" was not one any enlightened, well-meaning white Indianapolis resident would have considered using—did visit the museum.) But when the museum itself sponsored the organizing units—like the hobby and activity clubs—it was responsible for the racial makeup of the groups. Since other elements in the community had not yet prepared Indianapolis children (and indeed their mamas and papas) for groups involving black and white children, the guild responded to complaints from Negro teachers of discrimination by starting separate hobby groups for Negro children—for instance, a theater group, the Troubadors, and a Nature Study Club. Admirably, the February 1942 museum bulletin even featured a picture of Negro children happily involved in a hobby group. This was not to be a museum just for the grandchildren of board members or the children of guild members or of other Indianapolis families who had the time, knowledge and inclination to bring their children to a museum.

By the mid-1940s the schools were again strongly supporting the museum's classroom membership campaigns. Children's Museum campaign days were terrifically exciting to Indianapolis school children, who were given a feeling of strong proprietary interest in "their" museum when they exchanged their twenty-five cent dues for the familiar—and important—sea horse pin and membership card. As a matter of fact, at a 1944 museum conference, Mrs. Golden had been told that the museum's junior enrollment of nearly nine thousand was probably the largest in the country.

Mrs. Golden had continued to gain recognition, both within the museum field and in other areas. She had been elected to membership in Theta Sigma Phi, a college and professional women's journalism organization (now Women in Communications, Inc.), and more of her articles were being published in national magazines (*School Arts, The American Girl, Childhood Education*). In 1942, almost immediately after being named director of the Indianapolis museum, she had been elected chairman of the 5-year-old children's museum section of the American Association of Museums. Though national museum conferences were curtailed because of the war, in 1944, at the Midwest Museums Conference she was elected vice president for Indiana.

In the spring of 1945, there was a slight flurry of activity as Mrs. Golden informed the board that she was seriously considering an offer to become head of public relations and fund raising for Goodwill Industries in New York City. But her support on the museum board was strong. ("Mrs. Golden gave the usual excellent director's report," was a phrase often used in the board minutes.) She got along well with William Rockwood, and Mrs. Lilly ("Aunt Ruthie" to Nanci Golden) had become a close friend. Before Grace Golden left Indianapolis to visit New York for a final discussion with Goodwill, the board had increased her salary (to $3,500 annually) and agreed to send her to national museum conventions and to allow her time to study and advise other new children's museums. Said she, in her next director's report, "After your generosity . . . I am confident that, looked at from all angles, my job is the most rewarding in the city."

But the best was yet to come. With the war over, the museum could again turn its thoughts to finding a new location. Interestingly enough, a new building was now also greatly desired by the "mother museum," as the Brooklyn Children's Museum had been called six years earlier when children's museums all over the country had celebrated the fortieth anniversary of the first children's museum. In the early war years, representatives from the Brooklyn institution had journeyed on west to Indianapolis after attending a museum conference in Ohio. Their generous comments about the "wealth of excellent material you have collected" were very gratifying to their Indianapolis hosts. "I know of no children's museum which has such fine things, and we keep hoping that you will get your new building almost as much as we are praying for our own."

Another pass had been made at the Washington Boulevard residents in the early part of the decade to see if their opposition to having the museum as a neighbor had softened. It hadn't. In 1943, therefore, when the museum was offered $4,500 for the land, it snapped the offer up. (The land's value five years earlier at the time of Rockwood's gift had been estimated at $3,000.)

All the physical problems of the museum's quarters, so apparent before the war, had become even more acute. The filling station on the north side of the museum was sometimes cluttered with unsightly used cars, and the neighborhood was now not one in which women felt comfortable at night. (Mrs.

Golden had once struggled home on the bus carrying an awkward, gangling, night-blooming cereus plant so she wouldn't have to stay at the museum at night to see its spectacular, short-lived flowering.)

The building fund, consisting primarily of money from the Rockwood property, Mrs. Carey's bequest and the proceeds from the wartime waste-paper drive, received a healthy boost in December 1944. Mr. and Mrs. Eli Lilly gave the museum a $10,000 surprise Christmas present (asking, as was their custom, that the gift be announced publicly as "anonymous"). When museum benefactor William Rockwood died in 1945, memorial gifts in his memory were added to the building fund. (Rockwood also bequeathed the museum his large, excellent collection of Americana.)

Up until 1945, the museum had looked for property only south of Sixteenth Street, feeling that this would keep it centrally located for the public schools. However, it finally appeared that no suitable, affordable property was available within that boundary, and the search broadened.

At the board's meeting in December 1945, the building search committee announced that the St. Clair Parry home, a large limestone home, sitting majestically on the northwest corner of Meridian and Thirtieth Streets, looked like a good possibility. St. Clair Parry was a Laurel, Indiana, native who had come to Indianapolis in the late 1800s. He was president of the Parry Manufacturing Company, in which two of his brothers were also associated. The company, which made buggies, employed more than twenty-five hundred people in 1908. Later, as the Martin-Parry Corporation, the firm made car bodies. Parry was a financier, world traveler and student of international affairs. The property (actually two lots) on the corner of Thirtieth and Meridian had passed through many hands before Parry purchased it in 1911. The house he had built there in 1913–14 had a red tile roof and thirteen rooms, including a solarium and living room with a ceiling elaborately painted by a French muralist who had come over to work at the World Columbian Exposition in Chicago. Parry died in 1931, Mrs. Parry in 1945; the house at 3010 North Meridian was part of their estate.

The more closely the trustees examined and thought about the building, the better it looked. It was on bus routes and was centrally located. And though it was quite a bit smaller than the Carey house, it was situated so that additions, when they were needed, could be made. The carriage house at the back, which also was positioned so as not to interfere with future additions, would provide extra space. The neighbors were appropriate, too. On the north was the Rauh Library, a branch of the Indianapolis Public Library, housed in another former private home. To the south, across Thirtieth Street, was the magnificent former home of United States vice president Charles Warren Fairbanks. It had gracefully become the headquarters of Indianapolis Life Insurance Company, its exterior architectural beauty still carefully preserved.

The next few months were filled with negotiations, appraisals and a reorganization of the legal structure of the museum so that the trustees could have more freedom to borrow money. But the Children's Museum was not alone in thinking of the Parry house as desirable property. The Indianapolis Medical Society wanted the house as its headquarters, and an oil company was also interested in the property. Through the spring the bidding action increased. Finally, Indiana Trust Company, representing the Parry estate, sent a letter to all bidders announcing that, in order to be "equitable and fair to all prospective purchasers," a final auction would be held at the trust company's offices. It would continue "without recess so long as any bidder desires to make a higher bid."

Grace Golden was excited—and nervous—the morning of Monday, June 17, 1946. She wanted the property so much that earlier, when the medical group had suggested, informally, that the two organizations jointly share the property (the medical society to build on the corner lot), she instead tried to convince them to withdraw from the bidding. An oil company had already bid $61,250 for the property, topping both the earlier bids of the museum ($55,000) and the medical society ($52,500).

At 11 a.m. the museum contingent of Mrs. Golden, board president Jim Chase and first vice president Reily Adams (along with $7,000 in United States Treasury bonds as earnest money) were ready in the trust company's offices at the corner of Washington Street and Virginia Avenue. Also present were representatives of the other interested parties. The bidding began: $61,250 . . . $61,862.50 . . . $62,000 . . . $63,000 . . . $63,500. . . . It was the final bid, and it was from the Children's Museum.

The Medical Society, which quickly sent a warm letter of congratulations to the board of trustees, had never gone above its earlier bid of $52,500, partially because, as it explained in a newsletter to its members, it felt "constrained by the earnestness and needs" of the museum. The oil company also was said to have desisted "out of courtesy to the Children's Museum in view of its public and humanitarian character." For the first time in its history, the museum had a home of its own. Grace Golden was jubilant. That moment in the trust company offices, she was to say in later years, was a high point in her life.

CHAPTER TEN
3010 North Meridian

As bears go, this was not a large one—only 53½ inches from the tip of his ear to the bottom of the replica boulder on which his four paws were mounted. That put him right at eye level, however, for many young museum visitors. It was a momentous experience to come hurrying around the corner into a gallery and find yourself suddenly face-to-face with his yellow glass eyes and perpetually snarling mouth. This deliciously frightening encounter was the kind of thing you remembered when a grownup asked, "And what did you see at the Children's Museum this afternoon?" And like a ride on a roller coaster, it was the kind of wonderful scare that you were anxious to repeat on your next trip to the museum.

The black bear, his long fur dull from accumulated dust and coal soot, needed a thorough cleaning before he could move into his new museum home. That's why Children's Museum Guild President Isabelle Troyer, brush and bucket in hand, was spending a day out in the yard of the museum's new property at 3010 North Meridian. Much of the grime was soon removed from his black fur and honey-colored muzzle— and deposited instead on Mrs. Troyer. Being guild president, she was learning, was definitely not a white-gloves-and-tea-table sort of job.

Though most weren't in bad enough shape that they had to be taken outdoors to be cleaned, other museum exhibit pieces also were freshened up as they were transferred from the Carey house to the Parry house. Even the exhibits in the lending department had been refurbished. The museum workshop had built two hundred packing boxes, and it had taken the staff, occasionally assisted by grade school children, six weeks to wrap and pack the museum's thousands of cataloged objects. (Some additional material was to remain stored at the Carey house for the time being.) All through late summer and fall, carefully wrapped items were ferried to the new building, eighteen blocks north on Meridian, by the museum's station wagon (nicknamed *Hippocampus* —Greek for sea horse—said Filomena Gould in her newspaper column "Atop the Town"). A moving van transported the big pieces.

Meanwhile, carpenters and painters worked at the new building, converting its thirteen rooms into sixteen galleries. Museum staffers and guild members, in and out during the preparatory period, sighed as they realized that, inevitably, the living room's spectacularly decorated ceiling would have to be painted over with solid white, more appropriate for the room's new role as a museum gallery.

Before leaving the old Victorian building that had been its rent-free home for nineteen years, the museum's board of trustees paused to thank Mrs. Carey's family. To her "living daughters and grandchildren who have so loyally carried on with us in the spirit of your ancestor, we extend our thanks and ask for your continued good will," said the tribute of recognition, delivered at the October annual meeting held in the new building.

At last, in December 1946, the Parry house was ready to begin its new life as the Children's Museum. The date chosen for the opening, December 6, was the date traditionally celebrated as the museum's birthday because of Mrs. Carey's Museum Week, twenty-one years earlier. "And though it comes of age this December," wrote Mrs. Gould, "the museum has never lost its warmth, coziness, charm, its own brand of fey and child-like curiosity. A visit is to become entangled in its spell and without warning to become a child again."

For three special opening days, Indianapolis came to look over the museum's new home. Between five hundred and six hundred visitors came on both Friday and Saturday, and on

Sunday, a booming eight hundred. They saw a special, temporary exhibit of Spanish material collected by a Hoosier living in Spain, exhibits entitled "When Grandma Was a Girl" and "In Grandfather's Day" and a display of old-fashioned school books. They saw galleries of exhibits about Indians, China, Holland (with replica Delft tiles around a fireplace painted by a guild member) and Eskimos and the Arctic. They saw new fluorescent lights and closets that had been converted into cases by replacing wood doors with glass.

To some, however, there was a note of sadness to the occasion. Faye Henley, who had served the museum so long and faithfully, had taken ill and was unable to attend the opening festivities. Less than a month later, she died at age 79. She had been a trustee during the museum's entire twenty-one years and had held a variety of board offices, including a three-year term as board president when she was in her mid-70s. "Her vision and tenacity of purpose were a persistent urge that carried the museum through its tender formative years to its present gratifying growth," said the tribute from the board.

Miss Henley, having been so much a part of the museum's early, impoverished years, would probably have been amazed at the results of the fund-raising campaign for the new building. The accumulated building fund had taken care of $27,500 of the purchase price of $63,500. Board president Chase and campaign chairman John E. Hollett, Jr. had set $60,000 as a campaign goal: $35,000 to pay off the new five-year, 4 percent mortgage, and $25,000 for other moving and remodeling costs. (At one point, while the bidding for the Parry property was still going on, a $100,000 campaign had been considered—but only briefly.) In September 1946, trustees began making personal calls, and fund-raising letters were sent to all museum members, explaining in careful detail the museum's financial needs. The general public, members were told, would soon be asked to contribute, "but meanwhile our confidence rests in the ready response of our members to give now that rehabilitation may go forward. There will be no pressure, no expensive literature. We rest our case on past accomplishments."

The response was good enough for the museum to make the $5,000 payment, due on the mortgage, at the end of December, two months early. By early November, $7,867 had been given by 101 contributors; a month later, at the time of the December opening, the building fund had more than $35,000 in cash and pledges just from members of the museum. Both Block's and Ayres department stores contributed $2,000, and other retail firms followed suit. School children at fifty grade schools and two high schools staged special fund-raising events which produced a total of nearly $2,000 for the building fund.

In early June 1947, eight months after the campaign began, there was enough on hand to pay off the mortgage completely, but board president Chase recommended that only part be used for the mortgage and that the rest of the funds be retained for alterations and construction. By spring of 1948, a total of $70,000 had been put into the new building. But best of all, the museum was debt-free.

The museum was soon using its proud new quarters for important temporary exhibits, such as the two-month display of material from Angel Mounds, the fascinating dig down on the Ohio River presided over by the dean of Indiana archaeologists, Glenn Black. In addition to pottery, hair pins, ear ornaments, toys and other artifacts of prehistoric Indian life, the exhibit at the Children's Museum also included scale models of archaeologists' reconstructions of the village. Black himself spoke at a museum-sponsored lecture about his work.

There had been an interesting reaction from many Indianapolis citizens who were coming to see the museum in its fine new surroundings. They now perceived it as a safe, well-maintained repository for their personal treasures. Many new exhibit materials were coming in, to both the delight and despair of the staff, for there were increasing problems of storage to wrestle with. And that was even before the Children's Museum absorbed much of the contents of the Open Door Museum in Goodland, Indiana, a small farm community a few miles east of Kentland, in the northwestern part of the state.

For more than fifty years A. D. Babcock, a passionate collector, had filled tables, cases and boxes with Civil War swords, snowshoes, pewter cups, Roman lamps, early American household utensils, Indian jars, tomahawks, arrowheads, stone corn grinders, old books, flowers from the garden of Gethsemane and spears from the Upper Nile country (contributed by Babcock's Newton County neighbor, writer George Ade). His free museum opened to the public in Goodland in 1922. Its purpose, said Babcock, was to educate the boys and girls of the state.

Babcock's professions were ostensibly law and insurance, but the needs of the Open Door Museum always hovered around the edges of his business dealings. The back of his business envelope proclaimed, "I need your business and will appreciate it and will use every dollar I make above a living to build up and equip at Goodland the greatest museum in the United States. . . . Give me a chance to write your farm insurance and help the boys and girls of Indiana." A 1925 bulletin of the Indiana Historical Commission had called the Open Door Museum "perhaps the most unique museum in Indiana," and discussed its "large and valuable collection of Indian relics." Babcock died in 1934 at age 82. Thirteen years later his heirs gave the Children's Museum the Open Door Museum's collections, for "his desire was that children should have the benefit thereof," wrote his son James, an Indianapolis attorney, in a letter to Mrs. Golden.

One weekend in mid-1947, Mrs. Golden and daughter Nanci (who had joined the museum staff after finishing at Butler University) drove up to Goodland to view the Open Door Museum's four or five rooms-full of items and decide what the Children's Museum could use. A short time later Nanci and a couple of other staff members returned to the northern Indiana town to pack up the material. Using a couple of little boys hired on the spot (at a nickel a carton) to carry packed boxes out to a rented you-drive-it truck, the museum workers at last had the huge collection ready for the trip back to Indianapolis.

As the *Indiana History Bulletin* had stated earlier, the Indian artifacts were probably the strongest part of the Babcock collection. Yet among the very good—even rare—Indian pieces making the trip to the Children's Museum was an ordinary, visually unimpressive, 3½-inch-long damaged Comanche arrowhead. What set it apart from the thousands of other arrowheads, however, was that its history had been preserved. Typed onto paper, yellowed and ragged-edged with age, were the stark words of a long-dead Texas woman, Elizabeth Pinkerton Breeze, as she dictated them in 1916 to a Howard A. Michener, to whom she was entrusting the arrowhead:

Brother James was killed in September 1859. I was 15 years old at that time. It was about two o'clock in the afternoon. Mother and I were in the house patching and sewing and ran to the door. James was running toward the house and loading his gun as he ran. I could not see any Indians, but heard some yelling, and an arrow fell on the roof of the corn crib in front of the house. James was within twenty feet of the house when I heard the sing of a bow string and James fell right in front of me. The Indian had been hidden behind the corn crib. John Parker, who worked for us, saw the Indian when he shot James, and Parker shot and killed the Indian. We got James in the house. Mother and I cut his shirt off and we laid him on a bench face down. The place where the arrow was sticking out did not bleed much, but James was bleeding from the mouth.

By that time the neighbors were coming from all directions and they was shooting and yelling. James asked Pap to cut the arrow out of his back. Pap got his razor and I stood by James with a gourd of water. Pap cut a cross on James' back with the razor and took the shoemaker pincers and pulled the arrowhead out of the hole in James' back. He dropped the pincers and the arrowhead on the floor; that's how the arrowhead got the point broke off. Mother had James' head in her lap, but he was dead. The Indians never came back after that.

I was married in 1861 when I was 17 years old. My husband always lived with us from the time he was 3 years old. Pap and Mother raised him. His Pap, his Mother and three other older children was all killed by the Indians. Nobody knows how it was he was not killed. He was found beside his dead

Mother by my Pap. Pap brought him home and we always kept him.

I have always had that arrowhead ever since Pap pulled it out of James' back. Mother and Pap never did know what become of it. I never told them I had it. I had all of the beads and feathers and the bow and arrows that we took off the dead Indian that killed James. They have all been given away. My grandchildren got most of them, and I guess they are all lost. I wish you would someday give this arrowhead to some museum and tell them all about it. Give it to someplace where the people did not have it as hard as we did out here in Texas.

This chilling reminder of what life was really like on the American frontier (in museum custody, as Elizabeth Breeze desired) was given the accession number of 47.651.125. The first group of numbers (47) was the year it was acquired; the third group (125), the lot number or number for the entire "batch" of items (in this case the Goodland Museum collection); the middle number (651), the item number for this particular piece (the arrowhead). The cataloging at the Children's Museum, as at many museums around the country, was becoming more exact—and more complicated. This year/item/lot system had been installed in 1942. Before that time, the system had been a straight sequential one. As a matter of fact, when Arthur Carr had first come to the museum, he obtained from the Stout Shoe Store sets of numbers used to mark the left and right shoes in a pair. He would put one of the numbers on a museum item—often putting it right on the front—and the other on the item's catalog card.

Keeping the records of acquired items up-to-date had been a constant challenge to the staff, as it was to most museums. Carr, who had been so quick to criticize the museum's record-keeping deficiencies back when he had first taken over as Children's Museum director in 1926, later had found himself swamped. As he had told the board in the mid-1930s, "Through the years we have never had any assistance in such work and it has been quite difficult to keep up with the identification and classification, the cataloguing and acknowledging

This new home for the museum, designed by architect and trustee Kurt Vonnegut, Sr., was never built after zoning efforts failed.

Many examples of early furniture and tools, including the eighteenth century settle (rear, left) which was one of the early pieces given to the museum, were displayed in the pioneer kitchen gallery.

*Many museum-sponsored hobby groups met
in the upstairs activity room.*
W. Frank Jones photo

*Sewing groups were among the activities
organized by museum staff members and
volunteers for the city's children.* W. Frank Jones photo

The museum's aboriginal gallery.
W. Frank Jones photo

Young Tom Kahn and Tom Lugar were among those pitching in to help the museum move to its new home at Thirtieth and Meridian in 1946. Lugar would later become a museum trustee. Indianapolis Star-News photo

The St. Clair Parry house, bought by the museum in 1946, was the first building the museum ever actually owned.

The deteriorating old Carey house was finally torn down in 1948.
Indianapolis News photo

of the numerous accessions with other duties. . . ." After he turned over the directorship to Mrs. Golden, Carr had been firmly asked by the board to bring the accession files up-to-date "to give present location of these objects on exhibit and in storage," a chore he apparently had completed (and was paid for) by September 1942.

Carr, in fact, still buzzed about the museum, popping in and out from time to time, kibitzing on Mrs. Golden's operations. For his correspondence as Arthur B. Carr, Director Emeritus, he used a Children's Museum letterhead (with, however, his home address). Immediately after his retirement from the museum in 1942, Carr had been named one of fifteen directors of the William T. Hornaday Foundation, a new national organization which aided in the establishment of children's museums. In 1944 he became the foundation's president, and the Children's Museum sent him a letter of congratulations and a $10 donation for the foundation. In 1943 he was named an honorary life member of the Midwest Museums Conference, and, two years later, an honorary life member of the Children's Museum, for which he sent the board enthusiastic thanks. "It is beyond my capacity to express in full measure the great surprise and pleasure which your recent letter brought to me. . . ."

In the summer of 1946, following the temporary wartime suspension, a Prairie Trek expedition, the seventeenth, again rolled west to Cottonwood Gulch. The museum's board of trustees had decided that it was time to get its relationship—and, not incidentally, any potential liability—clarified and put down in black and white. Although the Prairie Trek had, of course, been associated with the museum for many years, the 1½-page agreement was actually the first official document that had existed about the "mutually beneficial relationship." In the brief paragraph describing the trek's commission, the document stated, "Indianapolis boys who are members of the Prairie Trek Expedition constitute an official field party of the Children's Museum. . . ."

The timing was ironic. Hillis Howie, who had just been named director of Community School, a private school in St. Louis, had been in New England since 1938 and director of school service at the Peabody Museum at Yale since 1942. Most of the twenty-eight boys on the 1946 Trek came from eastern and southern states, with only three on the roster from Indianapolis. It was the last summer that the Children's Museum flag flew above trek tents. In 1947, the expedition began using St. Louis as its home base.

Because the museum's new home contained less exhibition space, there was a more frequent turnover in displays. Of the sixteen galleries ready with displays for the museum's opening, only five remained the same six months later. The exhibits planned for fall 1947—on the British Isles, Scandinavia and Poland—were scheduled to coincide with social studies units in the schools. The front room on the north side of the marbled entrance hall had been transformed from the Dutch gallery into a nature center and work room for children, with plants, turtles and fish. There was also a "brag" shelf where children could proudly display the geodes, fossils and bird nests they had found. "Specimens are changed as rapidly as the seasons so that there is a feeling of life and movement," Mrs. Golden reported to board members at their March luncheon meeting at the Columbia Club. As for the museum's relations with nature on other fronts, inroads were being made into the long grass of the museum's ample front and side lawns (with the help of a donated, gasoline-powered lawn mower), and bushes and trees which had grown shaggy during the previous summer were being brought under control.

When Isabelle Troyer had taken over as guild president, she went in to see Grace Golden at the museum (as was customary) to ask her what she needed. "Money," came the one-word answer. Dances were reputed to be good ways to raise funds, so the guild staged its first one at the Indianapolis Athletic Club in November 1946. Using the museum's approaching twenty-first birthday as a theme, guild members made shocking pink (the color of the season) plaster birthday cakes as table decorations—the messy but modest firsts of what would soon become a tradition of guild dances, elaborate decorations. Guild members were very proud of the $1,000 they made on the dance.

A spring money-making event, sponsored by the board of trustees to help with the building fund, did even better. A May Market was held in the yard at the Carey house where all kinds of donations from museum supporters were sold—books, baked goods, furniture, fresh flowers in wheelbarrows, cherry tomato plants, even a Picasso print. Profits on the event were $3,051.07, even without the Italian mosaic paper knife which Mrs. Golden snatched up from the donated goods ahead of time, deciding it could better serve the museum as an exhibit piece in the new French, Italian and Spanish gallery.

As it turned out, this event was the last hurrah for the once-bustling and beloved old house at 1150 North Meridian. Carey Realty Company had asked that the museum finish moving out all of the material still stored there. Businesses now lined the formerly elegant residential street, and the Carey house was to be torn down and the land paved over as a parking lot. In June 1948, Mrs. Golden returned from the rarified, theoretical atmosphere of an international conference in Paris (the International Council of Museums) to a very specific museum-field problem. She was faced with the monumental job of checking through everything still stored in the Carey House, absorbing what she wished the museum to keep and somehow getting rid of the rest—all as quickly as possible. She was, in effect, between the rock and the hard place of Carr's years of never refusing anything, and the present reality of very limited storage at the new 3010 North Meridian facility.

The rest of the summer was spent in frenzied sorting. Some of the items which the museum didn't need and couldn't store were given to other organizations. A "branch" museum in a school in Lawrence, a township in the northeast corner of the county, took some of the surplus, for instance. The museum's gun collection, acquired during the period of Carr's directorship (inappropriate in a museum for children anyway, in Mrs. Golden's opinion), was lowered on ropes from a third-floor window, and most of the pieces were sold through gun dealers. Jars of preserved specimens were tossed onto a bonfire, with great cracking and sizzling as glass broke and alcohol ignited. Other material which Mrs. Golden found equally gruesome (like the two-headed calf and shrunken heads) plus things such as stacks of *National Geographic* magazines, were, according to museum legend, left in the basement as demolition equipment rumbled onto the property in September 1948. It would, perhaps, provide an interesting archaeological puzzle for some thirty-fifth century Glenn Black.

CHAPTER ELEVEN
Damascus Swords and Birds of Paradise

The design of a building can depend upon many things—budget, lot size, aesthetics. Seldom is the height of a giant ground sloth one of the determining factors. Yet the addition to the Children's Museum which opened in 1949 was carefully given a ceiling high enough so that a spectacular reproduction of a ground sloth skeleton could be mounted up on its back legs and heavy tail. In this position it was presumably nibbling tender tree leaves, a common activity for the huge, hairy, elephant-sized animals in the Ice Age days when they roamed over parts of America.

The museum's new addition was given the title of prehistory gallery. It connected the back of the Parry house with the carriage house, which, in turn, was converted into a natural history gallery. The ground sloth had been one of a group of a half dozen casts of prehistoric animals given to the museum two years earlier by Wabash College when its old science hall was dismantled. (Wabash president Dr. Frank Sparks was on the museum's board of advisors.) According to some accounts, the originals of the casts were in the British Museum. Before the new addition, there had been room to display only the smaller of the reproduction skeletons. But now, at last, the museum was ready for a borrowed derrick to hoist the reconstructed, eighteen-foot-long skeleton into place.

The ground sloth, its shiny ribs dangling high overhead like bars on a giant xylophone, was an instant child-pleaser. The newspapers, apparently operating on the theory that any big, extinct, prehistoric animal was a dinosaur, got off the track just a bit when reporting what this new, exciting thing was that the museum had. "Occupying the large area in the center of the new wing is Dinah the Dinosaur, a mammoth prehistoric mammal. . . ." said one newspaper account. Agnes Ostrom, in the *Indianapolis Times*, came closer: "A giant ground sloth skeleton, dubbed 'Dinah, The Dinosaur' by the children, dominates the center of the pre-historic gallery." Dinosaurs, technically reptiles, actually predated ground sloths, mammals, by about sixty-four million years. But who was counting? It was the kind of exhibit that young visitors headed for instantly when they came in the door. The Prehistoric Club was added to the museum's roster of after-school activities, and the museum guild used a dinosaur theme for its annual dance.

Elsewhere in the new gallery were other big plaster replicas: the shell of a glyptodon (an ancient, giant armadillo) and a mastodon skull. In cases around the edge were other exhibits about prehistoric animals and early humans, other assorted dinosaur bones, and another mastodon skull (real), as well as the plaster cast of the dinosaur footprint made by the Prairie Trekkers. On the walls were murals, painted by Indianapolis artist Tom O'Laughlin, depicting the glacier period and early man.

High above the cases on the north and south walls were wide bands of glass brick which admitted natural light, an idea Kurt Vonnegut, architect for the new addition, had used in the design for the building which had run into zoning problems on Washington Boulevard in the 1930s. "I know modern building techniques in museums tend toward artificial lighting, but in a children's museum we do not hold to this," said Mrs. Golden in a speech given later about the new addition. In fact, she had successfully talked the lighting contractors into cutting down the number of rows of fluorescent lights installed on the new gallery's ceiling.

Outside, the new addition was buff brick to harmonize with the carriage house and the rear service section of the house. Embedded in the wall on the south side was the museum's sea horse insignia, chiseled out of a block of limestone. The addition's cost was $35,000, financed in part by a twenty-year, 4 percent $20,000 loan from Indianapolis Life, the insurance company across the street. It was an "unusually low interest rate, offered as a neighborly gesture," trustees had been told at a board meeting.

Even as new exhibition space was added, the museum continued its activities in areas outside the galleries. Lending department display cases were supplied not only to regular school classrooms but to hospital children's wards and to the waiting rooms at juvenile court. During the spring, nature walks were scheduled in parks in various parts of the city. There were special-interest clubs after school every weekday; the best attended, surprisingly enough, was the Good Manners Club, at which some thirty grade school-age girls met "to acquire the art of being a gracious young lady at home and among friends." This could involve practicing the art of descending stairs gracefully or taking deportment field trips to other cultural institutions in town.

Mrs. Golden had been one of six Americans appointed by the International Council of Museums to work with UNESCO on museum problems. Following her attendance at a hemisphere UNESCO conference in Mexico City, a Mexican college student studying archaeology was brought to Indianapolis to spend three months as a visiting docent. The guild-financed program proved to be so successful that, in subsequent years, docents from Holland and Peru worked at the museum. Also added to the museum staff for a time was a talented glass blower, Frank Long, who had created a large display of glass insects while on the staff of the Carnegie Museum in Pittsburgh. A gallery on the history of glass was established, and visitors watched Long give formal demonstrations and painstakingly fashion small models of sea and plant life.

Through committee appointments (like the UNESCO project) and elective offices, Mrs. Golden was moving into positions of leadership on both the national and international museum scenes. In 1951, she was named president of the Midwest Museums Conference, the first woman to head that organization in its twenty-four-year history. When everyone who was anyone in the children's museum movement gathered at the Waldorf Astoria to honor the Brooklyn Children's

Museum auxiliary on its thirtieth anniversary, Mrs. Golden was one of seven speakers on the program.

Even in her earliest fund-raising days at the museum, Grace Golden had shown great talent as a public speaker. "Inspiring," some people had called her. Her skills—and popularity—on the speaker's platform continued to grow. During a two-month period following her return from Mexico City, she gave twenty-seven talks about the conference and "children reaching children" to an estimated two thousand persons, most of them teachers. Her other audiences ranged from the Indiana University Slavic Club (a lecture on folk arts) to Rotary Clubs in several states.

As chairman of the children's museum section of the American Association of Museums, Mrs. Golden delivered addresses at many professional conferences. Sometimes she shared with her peers specifics on how to develop good press relations. In other speeches, she described in detail the Indianapolis museum's use of the "storybook technique" in putting together an exhibit on Mexico. The exhibit focused on Carlos, a fictitious, city-bred Mexican school boy. "We acquired a handsome braided charro costume, boy's size," she told an audience at an AAM conference in California. "Because most of our remaining materials concerning boys are objects used in rural Mexico, the labels tell the story of Carlos' vacation visit to his country cousin, Pablo, who lives near Lake Patzcuaro. Pablo has a beautifully carved oxen yoke, he catches ducks on the lake with a boy-sized butterfly net and he hunts with a real atlatl. Thus we believe we achieve success in intriguing children, not only to look at the exhibit, but to read the labels by fastening their interest on a character."

Other times, her themes were more general: "The museum worker is trained to look backward, to measure the present in terms of the past." Or, "Today's youth is not so blasé that he is not awed by dinosaurs, sea life, Damascus swords and birds of paradise. It is our task to re-create the past, to focus attention on the out-of-doors, to dramatize the people of far off lands to make them come alive and draw the child within our doors . . . . The Children's Museum is not a settlement house, a play center or a zoo. It is a MUSEUM and its primary function is the meaningful display of objects."

The business about the zoo came from the heart. The Children's Museum had experienced firsthand the sometimes-unexpected results of having live animals as well as dead ones on display. With the expanded natural history quarters in the former carriage house, the turtles and fish in the aquariums had been joined by other small animals and reptiles such as hamsters, snakes and a pair of small caiman crocodiles named Pete and Repeat. One day a six-foot black snake, which had somehow gotten out of its cage and decided to investigate the front part of the museum, slithered through the pillared front entry hall and into the large south gallery. The resulting commotion when staff members spotted the runaway sent the snake scurrying for a safe hiding place—behind a steam radiator under one of the room's windows. No amount of coaxing or prodding could dislodge it. At last, Rosemary Skaggs, a young geologist from West Virginia who had joined the staff a year and a half earlier, turned the heat up in the radiator. As the pipes got uncomfortably warm, out came the defeated snake. Miss Skaggs quickly grabbed it and returned it to its cage.

For its thirtieth birthday party in December 1955, the Children's Museum came up with a particularly appropriate idea for invitations. Second- and third-grade school children who had recently visited the museum were asked to write the museum's adult members personal invitations to the museum's birthday party. Into the mail, along with a printed card from the museum containing the details, went three thousand letters carefully printed in pencil on lined grade school paper ("Dear Grownup, My museum is having a real birthday party. Everybody will have fun. Can you come? I hope so . . ."). Most of the letters contained colorful crayon drawings of a birthday cake, the ground sloth skeleton or some other, favorite museum item.

People were charmed by the ingenuous invitations, and, to their delight, many of the children received answering letters (and occasionally a donation check for the museum). More

than one thousand adults and children attended the celebration, and in honor of the thirty years, every thirtieth person
to walk in the door was given a door prize (with the hostesses
instructed to fudge the count enough to make sure the thirtieth
person was always a child). Invitations were also sent around
the country to others in the museum field. Among the replies
was one from the esteemed pioneer in the children's museum
field, Anna Billings Gallup, the first curator-in-chief of the first
children's museum (Brooklyn). "Little did I know children's
museums would multiply as they have," she wrote. "I am glad
our children's museums are creeping up into big money. It
took many years for human thought to realize what we were
talking about when we wanted for the country a new kind of
museum."

Also heard from was Arthur Carr, who sent "Greetings to
the Seahorse and its thousands of friends" from Florida, where
he and his wife had moved five years earlier. "We recall that
thirty years ago, Dr. Coleman [early board member Christopher Coleman] and Mr. Vonnegut meeting with the curator,
made the remark, 'This chile may die a-bornin' ' . . . . They
didn't then envision the splendid growth which in thirty years
has made the Children's Museum of Indianapolis, foremost of
them all." The letter, written in a spidery, slightly shaky hand,
was dated November 30. Thirty-five days later Carr died, at age
84. Said Mrs. Golden, in a biographical tribute, "He was so
completely devoted to the Children's Museum concept that he
gave far beyond what was required of him in hours and devoted service. [He] instilled in me and later in Mrs. Bell, who
was the third person to join our little staff, that care of material
is the first duty of a true museum worker. In these and count-
less others ways, he trained me and left lasting impressions
upon my life."

Having reached the ripe old age of 30, the museum was
now frequently confronted by those milestones of existence—
anniversaries and, inevitably, deaths. Kurt Vonnegut died in
October 1956, at age 71. His years of enthusiastic labors for the
museum arched back across the decades to 1925 and the first
board of trustees.

The perky little sea horse Vonnegut had designed for the museum in its infancy had a name by this time. "Sidney the Sea Horse," listed as editor of the newsletter that was sent to the museum's junior members, gave the young readers chatty information about the museum and upcoming exhibits: "Sometimes, late at night, when I am alone in the Museum, I start thinking about what a wonderful home I have. Occasionally, I get a little lonesome for my brothers and sisters in the ocean—but then I look around and see the fascinating historical things that are mine to see all the time, and then I start feeling sorry for my cousins in the ocean who only have each other."

In order that Sidney should not feel too lonesome, the museum had, from time to time through the years, tried to keep real sea horses in the natural science gallery aquariums. But the tiny creatures proved to be extremely difficult to keep alive in captivity. One of the problems, apparently, was duplicating their home water. That was why museum board president Jack Rauch (among others) found himself driving back from Florida with containers of genuine sea water fresh from Delray Beach sloshing around in the trunk of his car. Alas, the sea horses died anyway.

In a speech, Mrs. Golden had once called television "our greatest competitor for a child's time," but one which could "teach us much by new approaches." In the fall of 1954, Indianapolis children had a new weekly television program to watch on Monday evenings from 4:45 to 5 p.m. It was called "What and Where," produced by the Children's Museum. Nanci Golden, back in Indianapolis after taking a leave to go to Florida as organizing director of the Miami Junior Museum (and after a brief marriage to an archaeologist she met there), was selected to write and appear in the show. The choice was a natural one. Mrs. Golden's daughter knew the Children's Museum and its material; she had worked with children as a museum docent; and, most importantly, she had been a radio-television major at Butler University. The show was successful enough that the museum was asked to do a thirteen-week series on another channel, this time with a sponsor.

The sponsor was Union Starch and Refining Company of Columbus, Indiana, which was going to use the fifteen-minute program to advertise one of its product lines, the family of Pennant syrups. After turning down the idea for a junior quiz show, the sponsors decided they wanted something with an American heritage theme. An expensive set was built, depicting a cabin out on the old National Road. Miss Golden was to come out on the porch of the log cabin and greet children who came to visit, tell them some nuggets of history connected with the famous old road and bring out interesting artifacts from the museum's collection to tie in with the story of the day.

At last the program was ready for a run-through in front of the sponsors. That's great, they said. You've just given a plug to our biggest competitor, Log Cabin Syrup. The Pennant Children's Hour did run for thirteen weeks, featuring Nanci Golden and her Pennant kids (and the Pennant bird that said "Cheer up—with Pennant *Seer*-up"). The log cabin and its front porch, however, were carefully de-emphasized.

A man who had been an enthusiastic visitor to the museum vowed that the next time his boss was in town from the East coast, he was going to bring him by. As it turned out, one of the items in the museum that the out-of-town boss found to be particularly interesting was the director's daughter, and in January 1956, Nanci Golden and William McCollum, Jr., of Scotch Plains, New Jersey, were married. Unfortunately, shortly before the wedding, Mrs. Golden fell at home and broke her hip. With the mother of the bride in the hospital, guild members stepped in to complete the wedding arrangements, including those for an elegant little post-wedding luncheon at Mrs. Golden's house, catered by guild members. Wedding cake, champagne and other luncheon delicacies were taken down to Mrs. Golden in the hospital by guild president Mrs. John H. Compton.

Through the years, with the increase in activities of the Children's Museum Guild, being president of that organization had become almost a full-time job. Now, with Grace Golden temporarily out of commission, Mildred Compton found herself more deeply involved than usual in the day-to-day operations of the building at 3010 North Meridian. By April, Mrs.

Golden, hobbling a bit, was able to attend the monthly museum board meeting and take over the reins of the museum again, operating from a temporary office on the museum's first floor.

One of the activities that was keeping the guild busy was an ambitious project called the Craft Club. It had been the idea of Mrs. William Keller, who had prepared a home craft project for her children based on an Indian sand painting they had seen at the museum. Under Jo Keller's direction, guild members eventually were busy making components for several museum-inspired craft kits (a colorful Japanese carp banner, Chinese shadow puppet, Italian Christmas tree, Mexican fiesta mask) which children who subscribed to the Craft Club would be sent at intervals throughout the year. It was a clever idea and involved innumerable hours of planning and basement recreation room assembly-line work from guild members. Despite excellent local and national publicity (including an article in a March 1957 issue of *Life* magazine), national advertising and good sales to gift shops of other museums, financial returns from the project were never quite what had been anticipated. Remaining kits were eventually sold to a children's magazine, which used them as subscription premiums.

National publicity was again given to the museum with the publication, by its director, of two books for children. In 1955, Mrs. Golden had spent a month in Iceland, and in 1958, Alfred A. Knopf published *Made in Iceland*, one in the Knopf series of "Made In" books about the crafts of various countries. A *New York Times* book review called it "discursive and captivating" and its author "an authority on folk arts. . . ." Mrs. Golden's next book, however, was influenced by actual exhibit material in the Children's Museum.

In 1946, seven tiny dolls, made in Poland in the 1800s, were given to the Children's Museum by Miss Drucilla Cravens of Madison, Indiana. Ranging in size from 1¾ inches to 2½ inches tall, the little toys were carved from wood and decked out in colorful, painted military and folk costumes. The distinctive thing about them, however, was that each doll was supported on four boar bristles. When the dolls were set on a piano or organ and the instrument was played, the vibrations made it appear that the dolls were dancing. To someone with an eye for such things, here was obviously the stuff from which a good children's book could be fashioned.

But, interestingly enough, these were not the first items from the museum's collections to provide inspiration for a children's story. A set of unusual buttons, which had been on display in the Children's Museum, had provided the idea for *Matilda's Buttons*, published in 1948 by Lippencott. However, the author who had spotted these buttons and their potential was not Grace Golden, but Mabel Leigh Hunt, an Indianapolis writer of several children's books. This time, Mrs. Golden made sure that the dancing dolls stayed tucked away in their tiny oval wooden box and safely out of Miss Hunt's sight until her own book about them was well underway. In 1961, Bobbs-Merrill published *Seven Dancing Dolls*, by Grace Golden. Again the *New York Times* review was good. A "charming story of Poland . . . .the book hits its mark: it appeals to those for whom it is intended."

When Mrs. Golden was in Hungary in 1938 on the Carnegie Foundation fellowship, she had met a Hungarian political leader named Zoltan Horvath. He was interested in learning more about children's museums and had invited Mrs. Golden to spend several days at his family's estate near Budapest, where she met his wife and children. In 1956, with Hungary in turmoil after an abortive revolt against the Russian-controlled government, and with refugees spilling out of the country as fast as possible, Mrs. Golden found herself with an opportunity to repay the Horvaths' hospitality. The Horvath children, just youngsters at the time of her visit, were now adults with children of their own. Mrs. Golden was waiting at Camp Kilmer, New Jersey, to welcome Maria and Zoltan II, their spouses and children, when they arrived on New Year's Eve. As their American sponsor, she helped the two families find jobs and settle into life in Indianapolis.

In February 1958, the museum had yet another anniversary celebration, this time a tea following the annual meeting, honoring Mrs. Golden's thirty years with the museum. In her remarks thanking the board and members for a gold charm and their good wishes, she said, "It does not too often fall to the lot of any of us to have so long an experience of happiness and a sense of well-being in the job that brings one's livelihood." She was, she said, "proud to have brought the museum to its present position, and slightly humble, and agreeably expectant for the future."

CHAPTER TWELVE
New Girl in Town

As far as children are concerned," wrote Grace Golden in a letter, "a museum is not a museum without a mummy." For some time, the museum's director had wanted to fill this hole in the Children's Museum's exhibits. In 1953, the museum had displayed a mummy borrowed from the Wayne County Historical Museum in Richmond, Indiana. Now, she hoped to buy a mummy in London, Mrs. Golden told the board of trustees in March 1959, just before leaving on a four-week trip to Portugal to do research for another book in Knopf's "Made In" series.

Shortly before her departure, however, she contacted the University of Chicago's Oriental Institute, after reading a newspaper item about the institute's mummies. Much to everyone's delighted amazement, her call to the university resulted in the institute agreeing to send a mummy to the Children's Museum on loan. One Friday in May, museum trustee A. Malcolm McVie, in Chicago on business, paid a visit to the Oriental Institute. He was taken to a storage room and there, with the guidance of the institute's staff, selected the mummy and wooden case that seemed to be in the best shape. Scholars had determined from the markings on the case that the mummy was the daughter of a priest. She had lived in Egypt a thousand years after King Tut and several hundred years before Cleopatra, not earlier than the XXVI Dynasty (685 B.C.), and probably later. Her name was Wenuhotep.

During the second half of the nineteenth century, two German brothers, Heinrich and Emile Brugsch, were among the many European Egyptologists on the scene in Cairo and Luxor, Gizeh and Thebes, as knowledge about the country's rich past continued to unfold. Heinrich was the more famous of the two. He had helped excavate Memphis, and his specialty was deciphering ancient writings. Yet it was Emile who had been part of one of the most spectacular events in the saga of Egyptian archaeology. In the 1870s, when items of great value from ancient tombs mysteriously began to appear on the market, it was apparent that tomb robbers had found an important burial site that scholars so far had missed. At last the thieves were discovered, and in 1881, a representative of the Cairo Museum, Emile Brugsch Bey (this honorary title was often appended to his name) was sent to the valley of Deir el-Bahri.

Upon being shown the hole in the cliffs through which the robbers had entered, the intrepid Brugsch descended by rope down a deep shaft. At the bottom he was astounded to find rooms filled with the mummies of forty Pharaohs, moved by priests to this hiding place several thousand years earlier, to protect them even then from grave robbers. Brugsch was to witness something even more dramatic as the royal mummies were transported by river steamer from Luxor to Cairo. Word about the ship's special cargo had spread among the Egyptian villagers, and they lined the banks of the Nile, spontaneously filling the air with lamentations and performing other traditional rituals of grief, as their long-dead Pharaohs passed by.

It was this man, Emile Brugsch Bey, who was one of the links in the chain of events that would bring the mummy Wenuhotep to Indianapolis and the Children's Museum. Two patrons of the Art Institute of Chicago, Henry H. Getty and Charles L. Hutchinson, received from Brugsch Bey a large quantity of Egyptian material, which they, in turn, donated to the Art Institute in 1893. Among these items was the mummy Wenuhotep. In 1923 the institute published a *Handbook of the Egyptian Collection* and Wenuhotep was among the objects pictured and discussed. Sometime later, however, the Art Institute, which was expanding its collection of Far Eastern art, decided to divest itself of much of its Egyptian collection. One of the pieces that went, in 1941, to the Oriental Institute was Wenuhotep.

Down in Indianapolis, the museum's second-floor gallery (above the solarium) was being painted and otherwise made ready for the new guest. In early October 1959, the museum received a memorandum from Chicago: "We have forwarded today one box containing an Egyptian wooden coffin with mummy inside per Railway Express. . . ." Cautioned the letter, "The weight of the box is 445 lbs. so you will need some hefty help at your end." Though earlier the talk had been of a ten-year loan (and the mummy actually was still in residence in Indianapolis more than twenty years later), the first agreement between the Oriental Institute and the Children's Museum stated that the mummy was on loan for one year. Warned the autumn *Museum News, Junior Edition* , "If you want to see it, be sure you come soon, because we've only borrowed it from another museum for one year."

The mummy and the mummy case, of course, made a spectacular exhibit. A gold, cartonnage mask covered the mummy's face. (Cartonnage was the thin, papier-mâché-like covering placed over parts of the body.) Through the centuries, the mask's nose, damaged by time and travel, had become blunted. But the painted eyes, outlined in kohl-like black, still stared imperiously straight ahead. A cartonnage piece, decorated in red, blue, green and gold figures, covered the chest; another, covering the feet, had toenails of gold and sandal soles painted on the bottom. Where there were slight breaks in the neutral-colored linen wrappings, black discoloration from the bituminous preservative showed through. (This natural pitch was important to the etymological as well as the embalming process. Later-era Egyptians spoke of "pitch men," based on *mumia* , sometimes spelled *mumiya* , the Persian word for asphalt; hence, the word mummy.)

The wooden case was even more richly decorated. A vulture hood surrounded the carved face, which had been painted a vivid rose. The entire length of the case was decorated with registers (horizontal bands) of colorful figures with religious significance (Osiris, Isis, the Apis bull). Between the bands of decorative figures were columns of inscription, which identified the mummy as ". . . the august house-mistress Wen-uhotep, deceased, daughter of (the priest) . . . Thoth-hir-thaw" and "Her mother, the house-mistress Bast[. . .], deceased, revered in the presence of the great god, the lord of the sky." ("Hotep," a common element in Egyptian names, meant "to be peaceful or satisfied.") Several weeks after the exhibit went on display Mrs. Golden wrote to the Oriental Institute's director, "I cannot recall when anything has caused so much pleasurable interest. . . ."

The museum not only had a mummy at last, but financial conditions, such a trial in early years, had improved markedly. Lilly Endowment, which expanded the focus of its community giving in the late 1940s, had made its first grant ($1,000) to the Children's Museum in 1945. A few years later the annual amount was increased to $5,000, and then to $10,000. In 1955, after nearly 30 years of wooing off and on by various boards of trustees, the Indianapolis Foundation made a two-year grant, totaling $7,500, to the museum. It was for expansion of the museum's American history program.

When Lilly Endowment grants to the museum were increased to $5,000 in the late 1940s, the understanding was that they were to be used, at least partially, to improve the compensation of museum employees, including providing for pensions. A study of a pension program for Mrs. Golden was begun in 1949 under the direction of trustee (and insurance professional) Henry Peirce. Peirce, a museum trustee before the war, had been reappointed to the board in 1948, and was elected president, succeeding Jim Chase, in October 1950. Early in 1950, the museum began paying $1,800 a year on a refund annuity which would provide its director with retirement income. Modest hospital insurance benefits (for work-connected accident or illness) were obtained for all staff members, and the board agreed that employees could be placed under Social Security, should they so desire. A committee was established to study pensions for all staff members (though such a plan was not actually to be instituted for another fifteen years).

A modest attempt at obtaining corporate members was begun in 1954, and by 1955, one-third of the museum's operating funds came from members' dues, one-third from the schools and one-third from foundations. There were other gifts as well from museum supporters: for instance, property from the William H. Block family and money from Ruth Carey Haines (Mrs. Carey's last surviving daughter). Then there was the gift that would prove to be the keystone of the museum's endowment portfolio—10,000 shares of Lilly common stock, valued at $779,000, given by Mr. and Mrs. Eli Lilly.

But another old bugaboo had returned. The Children's Museum was popping out at the seams. A decade after the prehistory gallery addition, crowding—of visitors, exhibits and stored collections—had again become a major problem. As the museum had become better known, more and more material was being donated to it. Inevitably, the caliber of some of this was what was known in the museum trade as "On my way to the dump I thought of you." But much of it was well worth the room it would take to store it—if storage room could just be found.

Attendance told another part of the story. Back in 1947, at the time of the first annual meeting since the museum had opened in the Parry house, attendance for the preceding ten months was 35,000, exceeding the largest attendance in any previous twelve months by some 5,000. The prehistory gallery and remodeled carriage house had opened early in 1949, and attendance for that year was 45,462. Eight years later, in 1957, attendance for the year had climbed to 65,400, and the following spring, board president Jack Rauch appointed a special committee on expansion. In the summer of 1959, Tudor Hall, a private girls' school, was to move to a new facility on Cold Spring Road, leaving available its old buildings on Meridian, two blocks north and across the street from the museum. Trustees examined the school, but decided that another addition to the museum's present building would better suit its needs. In fact, architectural plans were already underway. The L-shaped addition was to be designed by architect—and museum trustee—R.F. (Pete) Daggett.

Though the original Parry property consisted of two lots, it was now becoming apparent that it certainly would be nice to have a little additional elbow room in the form of more land. At the rear of the museum's property was the Dreyer building, a commercial garage fronting on Thirtieth Street with apartments on the second floor. It was for sale, trustee president Jack Rauch announced at the board meeting in January 1959. A long discussion followed about the building's desirability and whether the museum could afford to make an offer. The feeling was that the 12,000-square-foot building could be remodeled as a new transportation gallery, as well as provide much needed space for work and storage and land contiguous to the museum's present property. The stumbling block, however, was money. The owners of the building were asking $60,000 for it—though the realtor thought it could be had for less. Mrs. Eli Lilly, the board's corresponding secretary, listened carefully to the long discussion but made no comments. A few days later, she told Grace Golden that she thought the museum should buy the building—and handed her a check for $55,000.

Architect Daggett was asked to figure out how the new addition could be extended west from the rear of the prehistory gallery (the Parry carriage house was to be torn down) and connected with the Dreyer building. Construction began in the spring of 1960. To get ideas for the addition's large new gallery, which was to be called the Hall of Man, Mrs. Golden and staff members Carl Armstrong and Estelle Preston Bell went to Chicago for four days to study the African and Eskimo galleries at the Field Museum of Natural History, just as Mrs. Golden had prepared for the prehistory gallery by going there eleven years earlier.

By the time of the next annual meeting in February 1961, enough of the construction was finished for members to have a sneak preview. The new facility, which almost doubled the museum's effective, usable space, consisted of the Hall of Man and new offices on the ground level, and craft rooms and a meeting room that would seat one hundred children on the basement level. There was also a new covered entrance way along the south side of the L.

There had been a change in plans, however. The part of the expansion that would have converted much of the Dreyer building into a transportation gallery was temporarily postponed when the money ran out. Back in 1960, Tom Billings, chairman of the museum's board of advisors, had been named chairman of the financial campaign fund and banker Wilson Mothershead (whose wife was secretary of the board of trustees) had been named chairman of the building fund. A goal of $253,000 was set. Challenge funds were offered by both Lilly Endowment and the Indianapolis Foundation, and by October 1960, the amount collected and pledged, combined with the amount already on hand, was enough to claim those funds. But in the meantime, the original plans for the addition had been expanded and costs had shot up. A year after the fund-raising campaign had been so optimistically kicked off, more money was still needed.

In June 1961, two months after the Hall of Man section officially opened, trustees were given new estimates of what it would cost to finish the Dreyer building conversion : $54,000 to remodel the south end and $16,000 to do the north end. It was decided to complete the work in stages, north end first. By November 1961, Indianapolis teachers were told in a membership letter from the museum that the construction work completed to date had cost $259,000 and was fully paid for. Donations were requested, however, for the final $28,000 work on the Thirtieth Street building. As a matter of fact, the board had decided it would have to go ahead and borrow $30,000 to complete the job. Mrs. Lilly again stepped in, offering to lend the board that amount—at no interest. (She was repaid two years later.) At last, on October 11, 1962, with the opening of the transportation gallery in the north end of the Dreyer building, the 2½-year building program was completed. The new facilities had tripled the museum's space.

Though the new wing and fund raising were taking much of everyone's time and attention, other museum activities continued along as well as possible, considering the construction dust and noise. Some dislocation was inevitable. Before it was all over, the 1,300 exhibits in the lending department—plus shelving—had been moved five times. Because of limited meeting space, Saturday classes for children were curtailed somewhat, and in 1960, and for the next few years, the museum closed for the month of August.

Torn up or not, however, the museum was still perking

with new people, new projects and new things. A Butler University student named David Cassady had joined the museum in September 1958 as a part-time clerk in the lending department; by 1959, he was also acting as docent. Cassady managed to keep interesting items—a shell, a fossil—in his desk in the prehistory gallery to discuss with the neighborhood kids who hung around the museum after school. Sometimes he would plan games in which they'd answer questions by examining various exhibits in the museum. Those who earned the highest scores were allowed to help with simple museum chores, such as stuffing envelopes or setting up rooms for programs. The response from the youngsters was so good (and the help of real value to the museum) that it was decided that the pick-up program should be formally turned into a service club called the Junior Docents.

In March 1961, the museum guild began publishing a monthly newsletter, and in the October issue there was important news about one of its own: former guild president Mildred Compton had joined the museum's staff a month earlier as "Mrs. Golden's trouble-shooter. She's to pop into any vacancy, take the pressure off wherever it's bearing down and generally be the leg 'man' for the museum," explained the *Guild Notes*.

There was another addition to the scene at 3010 North Meridian in the fall of 1961. A 130-year-old log cabin, one of the few authentic old cabins remaining in Marion County, had been offered to the museum two years earlier by Reily Adams, a long-time trustee, and also the husband of one of Mrs. Carey's granddaughters. The cabin had other Children's Museum connections. William Rockwood, the enthusiastic collector of Americana and the museum's benefactor in the 1930s, had originally moved the cabin onto land he owned north of town, land that later was purchased by Adams. Mrs. Rockwood, also a museum trustee, offered to give the money to move the cabin to the museum. Though experts determined that only its large main room could be salvaged, and that modern shingles, nails and chinking material would have to be used in its reconstruction, the cabin was moved, log by carefully numbered log, into the L of the museum's new wing. A new fireplace was built inside, and the log cabin was open and ready for visitors by September 1961.

Back in the 1950s, when museum board president Jim Chase had talked his law partner, Jack Rauch, into going on the board of trustees, he had given him a trenchant and illuminating explanation of how things happened at the museum. "A trustee's job," Chase told him, "is to implement whatever Grace Golden wants to do." Times change, however, as do boards of trustees—and directors, for that matter. Several members of the board began to feel that it was time for the museum to broaden its areas of interest—specifically, to do what some other youth-oriented museums in the country were doing: add a science gallery.

In 1958, Harley Rhodehamel, Jr., a former Prairie Trekker, son-in-law of 1930s trustee Benjamin Hitz and long-time museum supporter, joined the board of trustees. As a research chemist he undoubtedly paid more attention to science than did most people. But on October 4, 1957, all of America suddenly became more interested in science: Russia had launched Sputnik I. Seven months later, as plans were crystallizing for the addition that would become the museum's Hall of Man and transportation gallery, Rhodehamel suggested that the new plans include a science exhibit. Children, he explained "have a hard time conceiving what a scientist is and what it takes to become one."

Mrs. Golden conceded that some of the newer of the country's forty-five children's museums were developing science galleries but, she pointed out, such an exhibit required a trained scientist as a docent. To Grace Golden, gimmicky science exhibits, with children running around pushing button after button, held absolutely no appeal. The Children's Museum's strengths had always been in natural science and social culture. These, she maintained, should continue to be the perimeters of its programs and exhibits. There was no science exhibit in the 1961-62 addition, but, as far as some trustees were concerned, the idea was not dead.

There were other problems as well. For one thing, Mrs. Golden's health was not good. In 1957, two years after the fall which broke her hip, Mrs. Golden had again been hospitalized, this time because of a heart attack. Since then, several flare-ups, apparently caused by her heart, had occurred. Things at the museum were beginning to slide a bit. Part of the problem was that Grace Golden had always controlled everything herself. She decided where the walls of a new addition would go. She approved every exhibit label written. "Grace very much ran her own ship. She had lieutenants; she didn't have an executive officer," said one observer of this period. And with failing health (which double-martini lunches at the Driftwood Room of the nearby Marott Hotel did not help) and the expanding size of the museum, it was increasingly hard for her to handle everything personally.

Yet it was a drum used in the funeral cortege of John F. Kennedy that was the straw that broke the camel's back. It was a replica Revolutionary War drum, and Tom Billings had made arrangements, through contacts in Washington, to have the drum go on temporary display at the museum. Mrs. Golden was furious. Not only was the exhibit not arranged through proper channels (this had happened before with Billings' brainstorms), but the drum would bring with it the aura of tragedy and death. These, insisted Mrs. Golden, were absolutely not things that should be emphasized by a museum for children.

Things came to a head after the February 1964 annual meeting. The trustees also favorably discussed putting up a museum sign on Meridian—something that Mrs. Golden also did not want. And Billings was re-elected chairman of the board of advisors. A week later, Rhodehamel, who had taken over as board president the year before, went to the museum at Mrs. Golden's request. After a brief, amiable chat about her ideas for expanding the museum's staff library, Mrs. Golden floored him by announcing that she was tired and fed up and had decided to resign. Some felt that, perhaps, this was just a power play; others (including her daughter, Nanci) felt she genuinely wanted to retire.

In succeeding days, when Mrs. Golden refused to come back to her office, Rhodehamel polled as many trustees as possible by phone and the rest of the staff in person and found them agreeable to Mildred Compton being named acting director. (Ironically, Mrs. Compton had decided some months earlier to leave the museum, but had promised Mrs. Golden she would stay until the end of the school year.) At the March board meeting, Mrs. Golden (who was on a trip arranged earlier to Yucatan with daughter Nanci) was granted an indefinite leave of absence. A month later, at the April 15 board meeting, Mildred Compton, 47, was chosen as the new director of the museum. Officially, her new title would become effective in mid-June. Unofficially, her duties began immediately.

At the same meeting, Grace Golden's poignant letter of resignation was also read:

Dear Harley and all Trustees:

After nearly thirty-seven happy years, I request my retirement as director, effective, as you suggested, on June 14, my 65th birthday.

A trying fact in all museums is that it is a rare day when all work is finished. Ours is no exception. I shall be glad, whenever asked, to consult on anything left undone . . . if I am needed. . . .

I have fully enjoyed my contribution in bringing the Children's Museum to this point and have been richly rewarded through the years. It falls to few people to be so blest in their day to day tasks.

At the risk of sounding like a sentimental old fool, I quote my favorite 16th century Portuguese sage:

I weep not because we have parted,
Only that no one will ever love you as well.
Be of good cheer!
(signed) Grace

CHAPTER THIRTEEN
Road from Bicknell

Mildred Sartor Compton had no particular intention of ever becoming a museum director. On the other hand, Mildred Sartor's mother had every intention that her younger daughter (and her older daughter too, as far as that was concerned) would become something other than the wife of a Bicknell miner (or even mine executive), or farmer, or tradesman, or any other young man tied to life in this small, grimy, southwest Indiana town.

For Bicknell, Indiana, was a coal town. Yet it was good farm land, not coal, that brought the first Sartor, George Washington Sartor, to this area northeast of Vincennes in the early 1800s. The first mine was opened in 1875, and by 1917, when the Sartor's second daughter was born, most people just shrugged and accepted the film of coal dust that covered the narrow streets and small frame houses of the workers on the outskirts of town.

For the next decade particularly, the little town boomed. By 1926 there were fourteen mines in the Bicknell fields, including American Number One, one of the state's largest deep mines. And if the good people of Bicknell couldn't be particularly proud of the appearance of their little town, at least they could be proud of American Number One. On the first Saturday in June, 1926, straining, sweaty workers, their tired eyes white spots in coal-blackened faces, hoisted from the mine a staggering 7,157 tons in just eight hours. It was a new world's record. And though it was the fourth such world record achieved by American Number One, it was an event still worth discussing at Bicknell supper tables. (In Bicknell homes, as in those in most Indiana small towns, dinner was the meal served at noon.)

Not that American Number One and its world-record disgorgings mattered all that much to 8-year-old Mildred Sartor. Her father, after all, was not a miner. But in a way, his business, too, was coal. He was a banker, and the economic conditions of the coal mines—the strikes as well as the records—affected the Sartor household at 704 West Fourth Street just as they did the households of miners. Noble P. Sartor was a founder and president of Bicknell Trust and Savings, and in 1929 and the years following, when the United States fell apart financially, his bank, like banks all over the country, was engulfed in a tidal wave of panic. As historian Samuel Eliot Morison would later write, "Queues formed outside perfectly sound banks, on a rumor, to withdraw deposits, and any run on a bank forced it to close its doors."

On the day that this finally happened to Bicknell Trust and Savings, the bank filled with frightened folks milling about, frantically demanding their money. Sartor climbed up onto a desk top so he could be seen as well as heard. The angry faces he looked down into didn't look like the faces of friends and neighbors he had been doing business with for years. But they believed him when he said they would all get their money. Sheepishly, the customers left. The run on the bank was stopped. And it was always a point of pride with him that after the bank moratorium closed the banks in early 1933, Bicknell Trust and Savings was the first of the town's three banks to reopen.

At about this time, Mildred Sartor was finishing high school. Her mother had successfully forestalled any entangling alliances which could keep her obviously bright, capable young daughter from seeing what life was like outside of Bicknell. Only three in the high school's class of sixty-six were going on to college. For Mildred Sartor, the first choice would have been the University of Michigan, which she had seen many times on family trips to visit relatives in Ann Arbor. But Dora Sartor was realistic about the academic preparation her daughter had received in the Bicknell schools. Instead, to introduce her to higher education and to "soften the edges a little," young Mildred, only 16, was sent off to a two-year girls' school, Ward Belmont Junior College.

Two years later, when she at last did enter Michigan (as a junior), Millie, as she was now called, appreciated her mother's foresight. Michigan was not only Big Ten, but big classes and big academic competition. The good student who had easily sailed through small-town Indiana schools and junior college suddenly found herself, for the first time, really having to study. The first semester was rough for the chemistry major, even if she was living in an upper-class honor dorm. The tall, willowy brunette was also one of only three or four girls in the chemistry school, which meant a busy social life—a big change from Ward Belmont where an eagle-eyed chaperone was always required on those rare occasions when dates with boys were allowed. Of the thirty students in 1938 who received a Bachelor of Science in Chemistry degree (an academic step up from a plain Bachelor of Science degree), only two were girls. The other one was from Russia.

Graduate school was now the goal, but the lingering effects of the Depression were still affecting the Sartor family pocketbook. And then a solution presented itself. On the recommendation of her organic chemistry professor, Millie Sartor was hired as a graduate instructor at Sophie Newcomb college in New Orleans, the women's part of Tulane University. This, in turn, made it possible for her to work for a master's degree in chemistry at Tulane. Graduate studies went well; teaching, however, was less professionally rewarding. Freshmen southern girls tended not to be science-oriented. "How much do I have to learn to pass?" they frequently wanted to know.

But even this exposure to the southern-belle mentality was part of a non-classroom education that Millie Sartor was receiving in New Orleans—an education in the world of culture, charm and gracious living. And the "professor" in this extracurricular education was her landlady, a wealthy widow who lived three blocks from the university and kept students in her home so there would be some young company around for her high school-age son.

Mrs. Dunwody was interested in a wide range of civic projects. She had been chairman of the first Sugar Bowl Stadium drive, for instance. Soon Millie Sartor, like the two medical students in the apartment downstairs, was calling her "Granny." Part of Granny's curriculum consisted of making sure that her young tenants attended whatever important events were going on in town. She would buy tickets and then announce, "We're going"—to a play or a performance of the touring Metropolitan Opera Company.

It was 1939, the year the movie "Gone with the Wind" was released. After attending a performance with Mrs. Dunwody, the three boarders all came home fascinated by the life of the Old South the film depicted. The evening concluded in great hilarity in the Dunwody parlor, with lessons on how to curtsy from Granny, who, despite her years, could still drop a curtsy as smoothly and graciously as Scarlett O'Hara herself. The little girl from Bicknell, Indiana, had indeed shaken the coal dust from her shoes.

There was never any real question about what Mildred Sartor would like to do with her chemistry degrees. Her goal was a job with Eli Lilly and Company. Even while she was still in Michigan, she had visited the Indianapolis headquarters to discuss future employment. The people there were polite and noncommittally encouraging. On her next visit a year later, the employment director suggested she consider graduate school. During the summer after her first year at Tulane, she made a third trip to the red brick building on McCarty Street. This time, she was taken across the street to meet research department director Harley Rhodehamel, Sr., who could evaluate the abilities of this persistent young woman with good academic credentials who wanted to join Lilly's research department. The timing was fortuitous. With the completion of an addition to the research building scheduled for early 1940, the company was indeed going to have an opening for another organic chemist. Could Miss Sartor, Rhodehamel asked, finish at Tulane a semester early?

She returned to New Orleans, dropped the teaching assistantship so she could devote more time to her master's thesis and went to work for Lilly in early 1940, the only woman in organic research. (There was another woman in biological research.) We don't usually hire women, she had been told during her earlier interview, because it takes five years for an employee to be really productive in the research lab. "I'll stay five years," promised chemist Sartor. She ended up staying seven.

At first, much of the lab work she did was on projects begun by research department head Horace Shonle, who, because of the administrative load he was now carrying, was able to spend less and less time himself in the lab. Later research projects in which she was involved concerned stilbestrol and a brand new group of substances called antihistamines. Several summers, young Harley Rhodehamel, on vacation from Purdue where he was a chemistry major, worked at Lilly, taking up residence at a lab bench across the hall from Mildred Sartor.

It was not all work for Lilly employees. One of the most popular of the company-sponsored recreational groups was the Lilly Skating Club, which met Saturday mornings at the State Fairgrounds Coliseum. It was a popular activity for both single employees and those who were married and brought along wobbly-legged youngsters who determinedly made it around the large indoor ice rink, clinging desperately to the sides. The club was a natural for Millie Sartor who had done a lot of ice skating while going to college in Michigan. She was a good skater. So was the tall, sandy-haired young man who introduced himself and smoothly skated with her around the rink at one of these Saturday-morning sessions in 1940. One of the reasons for such company-sponsored clubs was, of course, to help employees become better acquainted. For John Compton, an Indianapolis native and 31-year-old employee in the Lilly purchasing department, and 23-year-old Millie Sartor of the organic research department, the club indeed served its purpose.

But war years impose their own timetable on romance. In the early 1940s, this was discovered by all young men and women who were meeting and skating and sipping hot chocolate and dancing. In 1942, Compton went into the army with a commission as a medical purchasing officer. Like many young men, he was eager to get overseas, to get into "action."

Yet at Christmas time 1943, Compton was still in this country. And it looked, he said when he came home on leave, as if his unit would continue to remain in the States. Why not go ahead with wedding plans—a June one, at the Sartor home in Bicknell?

Surprising news was awaiting Compton when he returned to his base in North Carolina. His medical unit was on alert, preparing to be shipped overseas the first of February. Instead of a June wedding in Indiana, there was a January wedding in North Carolina. The bride-to-be and assorted Sartor kin journeyed down to Camp Buckner for a ceremony in the chapel. After a brief honeymoon, the new Mrs. Compton returned to Indianapolis and her work at Lilly. She worked in the Lilly research labs two more years, resigning in August 1946. Baby Sara Compton was born the following December.

The Compton family settled easily into the domestic suburban life relished by young couples the country over in the postwar years. In 1948, a boy was born and named John for his father. The Compton house on Kingsley Drive was in a handy location for several reasons. Just a few blocks away was Broad Ripple Park, with its swings, slides and still-operating (though sadly deteriorating) carousel. It was a fine place to take the children on warm summer afternoons after their naps.

The neighborhood also turned out to be particularly handy for John Compton, for there were enough Lilly employees in the vicinity that a car pool was formed. One of the men in the car pool was George Varnes, who would one day play an important role in Children's Museum affairs. The fellowship of the men who journeyed back and forth together every day developed into family friendships, and the Comptons and the Varneses and other couples spent enjoyable evenings together at dinner parties and other neighborhood get-togethers. The friendships survived even when many of the families began moving out of the neighborhood and into larger homes in other areas.

Like many conscientious young mothers eager to expose their children to places and events that would help expand their knowledge, Millie Compton decided it was time for her children to visit the Children's Museum. She herself had never

Museum trustees Evan Walker,
Kurt Vonnegut, Sr. and James R.
Chase look at exhibit material in a
new gallery in the Parry house.
Indianapolis Star photo

The pergola at the rear
of the Parry house was
often used for outdoor
nature classes, such as
this one being
conducted by director
Grace Golden (rear).

A reproduction of a ground sloth skeleton was a particularly popular feature of the prehistory gallery, added to the museum in 1949.
Indianapolis Star photo

Children's Museum Guild members who gathered by the front door for a newspaper photograph publicizing the guild's 1949 fall fashion show were Mrs. Frederic M. Hadley, Mrs. Frank T. Sisson, Mrs. William T. Finney and Mrs. Dale E. Stenz.
Indianapolis Star photo

*Staff members Estelle Bell and Nanci Golden unpack
new acquisitions for the museum.*
Filmcraft photo

The mummy Wenuhotep went on display at the museum in 1959.

Teenagers in the 1950s check out the museum's
famous Black automobile.

After twenty-two years as
director, Grace Golden retired
in 1964.

been there and knew nothing at all about the place. She found the building at 3010 North Meridian filled with school children, and most of the exhibits turned out to be for children older than the toddler and preschooler she had in hand. Perhaps, she thought, she had brought them a bit too soon for them to appreciate the things they were seeing. Yet the children themselves enjoyed it, and they all came again.

As the children got older, Millie Compton got involved in community volunteer activities—P-TA work at School Eighty-four and the neighborhood Cub Scout den, for instance. One of the little boys in her cub pack was Steve Sullivan who lived across the street and was a good friend of Johnny Compton's. Twenty years later he would be manager of finance and operations at the Children's Museum.

In the spring of 1952, Mrs. John H. Compton, 5420 North Delaware, received a handwritten note informing her that it was with great pleasure that she was being invited to join the Children's Museum Guild. With equally great pleasure, she accepted. Each spring the women's pages in Indianapolis newspapers bloomed with photos of socially impeccable young matrons who were joining various leagues, guilds and auxiliaries. Millie Compton dutifully posed with nine other young women in a photo for the June 7, 1952, *Indianapolis Star.*

The new members soon learned that women who belonged to the Children's Museum Guild did a lot more than get their pictures taken for the newspaper, however. Not only did they stage a variety of events to raise money for the museum, but they were expected to spend a considerable amount of time helping at the museum itself. One of the first items on the itinerary of a new guild member was an orientation tour of the museum led by director Golden. To Millie Compton, walking in the massive, old, front doorway for the first time as a guild member, the museum seemed totally different from when she had visited it earlier with her children. As she looked at the exhibit case in the front hall, she thought, "I am going to enjoy being a part of this rather than an observer." That day was also her first meeting with Grace Golden.

Guild members were required to spend thirty-five hours every year in museum-related activities. Many of Mrs. Compton's guild hours in the next few years were spent making dance decorations—sprinkling glitter on cardboard angels or assembling dyed chicken feathers into brilliantly colored fans. Then, too, there were the Sunday afternoons at the museum, staffing the desks and answering questions about the giant skeleton (no, it's actually a ground sloth, not a dinosaur) and the direction to the rest room (downstairs, turn to your left).

In the spring of 1955, three years after joining the organization, Mrs. Compton was elected president of the guild. Shortly afterwards, she was walking down the steps into the museum's prehistory gallery just as Grace Golden came walking through. Their contact had been minimal to that point, for Mrs. Golden was not in the museum on Sundays when guild members did their volunteer stints. To Millie Compton, she had always seemed quite formidable—and the tone of her first greeting was not particularly reassuring. Said Mrs. Golden, very stiffly, "I'm glad to meet you now that you're going to be president." The tone and manner were enough to make Mrs. Compton wonder if, perhaps, the museum director had not entirely agreed with the guild's selection of a new leader, though normally it was a process into which Mrs. Golden had much input.

However, the stiffness quickly relaxed into a good working relationship, and they soon knew one another very well indeed. In any year, the guild president and the director always spent a great deal of time working together. When Grace Golden fell and broke her hip, Millie Compton was drawn even more closely than normal into the actual running of the museum. (In fact, she was even admitted into that select circle of those who were invited to call Mrs. Golden "Gigi.")

Once the guild president's official year was over, she was usually asked to continue handling some duties for the museum. After all, so the thinking went, she—and her family— were conditioned to her spending much time on museum matters. Why not quickly run in something else before that time got reabsorbed by bridge games or work for another volunteer group? And Millie Compton, never particularly the kind of person to stay home and do housework, was ready to stay active. The job Mrs. Golden had in mind for her was making calls on township school superintendents as part of an expanded campaign to get financial support from the burgeoning township school systems, like that provided by the Indianapolis city schools. Mrs. Compton also began attending the series of classes the museum director was conducting as part of a program to turn guild volunteers into trained docents.

But events in her personal life cut short the docent classes and, for a few years, her involvement with the museum. In 1958, John Compton had his first heart attack, and three years later, in June 1961, at the age of only 50, he died. During those three years, knowing that there was a chance that she might need to go back to work, Millie Compton had returned to school (Butler University) at night to get a secondary license to teach chemistry. Now, upon his death, she fully expected to become a high school chemistry teacher.

Grace Golden, however, had a different idea. When she was unable to reach Mrs. Compton by phone (she was not taking any calls), Mrs. Golden sent a guild member to her house with the message that Mrs. Compton was to get in touch with her before making any decision. A few weeks later, after getting the children off to camp and spending time with her family in Bicknell, Mrs. Compton met Mrs. Golden, board president Jack Rauch and treasurer A. Malcolm McVie for lunch. Both men had been impressed with Mrs. Compton's work when she was president of the guild and working closely with the board of trustees. Mrs. Golden said she'd like for Mrs. Compton to come to work at the museum. But the pay was not very good, and with the responsibility of young children, Mrs. Compton knew she must think carefully about this decision.

She turned for advice to Edward Kassig, head of the chemistry department at Broad Ripple High School where she had done her practice teaching. "If I were you," he said, "I'd give it a try." High school chemistry teachers are so hard to find, he told her, "that you can always get a teaching job up until the day before you're 65." That helped make the decision. Also, Mrs. Golden was agreeable to her working short days so she could be home when her children got home from school. Her title was to be executive secretary, the same title Grace Golden had used in her early days at the museum.

Among other things, Mrs. Compton was put in charge of the school membership campaign. This job included tabulating the endless, handwritten lists of twenty-five-cent and $1 school memberships. The record system sometimes involved days of tracing teachers through changes of schools, changes of names—all for $1. Mrs. Compton also got her first lesson in accessioning when she was asked to help Estelle Bell catalog a diverse collection that had been given to the museum by a travel agent. But in addition to lessons in professional museum procedures, there were frustrations. Mrs. Golden did not easily delegate responsibility. She also was not particularly open to new ideas from her staff, Millie Compton felt. "I understand how you feel," Mrs. Golden would tell someone who had come to suggest a change, "but you must believe me, there are reasons why we do things the way we do."

Yet during the days at the museum there was time for long talks—reminiscences. Mrs. Golden would tell Millie Compton about her early days at the museum, about its history, about trustees with whom she had worked. And all of this—an appreciation of the museum's past and remarkable growth under Grace Golden, a growing knowledge of its present strengths and weaknesses—began to give Millie Compton a glimmer of what its future could be.

CHAPTER FOURTEEN
Boo!

Ⅰt was serendipity, really. The St. Louis hotel was jammed with delegates to the May 1964 convention of the American Association of Museums. Among them was Mildred S. Compton, brand-new museum director attending her first AAM meeting. Yet out of all those hundreds of people, Millie Compton found herself riding down the elevator one morning with a man she'd always had some curiosity about, but had never met.

His name was Julius Carlebach. It was a name familiar to many museum directors, and Grace Golden had talked of him often. Someone had pointed him out to Mrs. Compton earlier during the convention. He was a dealer from New York City whom Mrs. Golden had known since he fled to New York from his native Vienna when the Nazis took over. "Our dealer friend in New York," she had called him in her annual director's report in 1961.

And he was, perhaps, as much friend to museums as dealer through whom they bought and sold things. If he wasn't able to sell something for a client, he might well suggest that the client donate it to a museum—and, of course, receive the tax benefits thereof. In 1960, for instance, "New York City patrons," through Carlebach, had donated to the Children's Museum nine pieces from Egypt and the South Pacific, appraised at $1,285. "Although he has never been in this museum, he is its staunch friend," Mrs. Golden had told the board.

As the elevator approached the lobby, Mrs. Compton introduced herself to him, told him that Grace Golden had retired and that she was the new director of the Indianapolis Children's Museum. Was she, he asked, going over to the special May Company "grab-bag"? Morton May, head of the retail company, had decided to dismantle his large collection of New Guinea primitives. He had divided the items into several groups, and museums were being allowed to select a limited number of pieces from each group on a first-come basis. She told him that she was, but not until later in the day.

"Go now," he said firmly, and walked away. This left the Indianapolis contingent—board chairman Harley Rhodehamel, David Cassady, now director of the education department, and Mrs. Compton—in something of a quandary. They were all, they realized, babes in the woods when it came to making shrewd, fast, ethnologically sound decisions on what to select. After a hasty conference, it was decided that Cassady should go.

He returned a few hours later, delighted with his fourteen selections, among them a large, half-moon-shaped shield with tassels from the Sepik River region. His morning's work, in fact, doubled the museum's New Guinea collection. (The May pieces were later appraised at $1,100 to $1,300.) Mrs. Compton never met Carlebach again.

The museum they returned to in Indianapolis was healthier than might have been expected, considering the recent trauma at the top. Attendance was running about six thousand visitors ahead of the year before. Memberships in all categories had increased, though one of the year's priorities was to push for more corporate members. The museum had no indebtedness.

As the news of Mrs. Golden's retirement was officially announced to the community, the newspapers blossomed with tributes. "Ceremonies and parties may honor her retirement but this lady can never really quit her job," editorialized the *Indianapolis Star*. "So long as children walk through the rooms and galleries of this unique museum, Mrs. Grace Golden will be contributing. . . ." She had, of course, been well-thought-of by many newspaper people in town. She knew what sort of material newspapers needed to make readable stories, and she had seen to it that they got it.

At the retirement festivities at week's end, there were a few awkward pauses and forced smiles over dinner tables and in receiving lines, but on the whole, all went more smoothly than perhaps might have been expected. To the outside world, the museum family was presenting a united front. Some three hundred civic leaders, newspaper people and others turned out on June 10 for a late-afternoon reception at the museum at which Mrs. Golden received a gold disk proclaiming her a member of the Order of the Golden Sea Horse. It was the same award Arthur Carr and Faye Henley had received in earlier years.

Afterwards, board president and Mrs. Rhodehamel had a small dinner party in her honor, and the next night, the board and past presidents of the guild entertained at an elegant cocktail buffet featuring boned turkey stuffed with forcemeat, leg of lamb and tenderloin in aspic. The decorations, the newspaper women's pages breathlessly reported, were geranium topiary trees and Shasta daisies. All of that concluded, Mrs. Golden went off to New Jersey to visit her daughter and granddaughter. At the trustees' meeting the next week, it was announced that she would receive monthly retirement benefits of $300 from the museum, plus another $300 from insurance, social security and "other benefits."

Not surprisingly, the image of Mrs. Golden peering over their shoulders, approving or disapproving, was still with museum staff members to some extent. The controversial drum went on display at the museum later in June. Mrs. Compton and Mrs. Golden had been carrying on a correspondence that was very cordial in tone on both ends, and in her next letter, Mrs. Golden mentioned the drum. "Saw the drum picture in the *Star*, which I take here," she wrote. "It did look like a beautiful piece of workmanship."

Replied a relieved Mrs. Compton, "Oh Gigi, I'm so glad you know about the drum. We didn't want to upset you—but I'm certainly relieved that you know about it. It is really a very interesting and unusual drum. . . ." And, she added, it seemed as if all the men on the board had been in to see it.

Museum life continued on other fronts. A new front door with required panic bar was installed. New sod was laid on the banks in front of the museum, and, in turn, new, healthy-lawn equipment was purchased to care for the new, healthy lawn. New stationery featuring the sea horse was designed by Indianapolis ad man (and museum trustee) Ray Sweeney. The prehistory gallery was renovated. An electric typewriter was purchased. Two lending cases, accustomed to traveling no farther than to Indianapolis schools, instead were sent off to the American Museum of Britain, in Bath, which wanted to use them as models for a lending department it was establishing in England.

In August, while the museum was closed, books were gathered up from closets, the tops of filing cabinets and the corners of desks and put all together in a room on the north side of the first floor. A library table and chairs were added, and at last, the staff had a room set aside just as a library. Registrar Bell, who had been in that room, moved upstairs to more spacious quarters.

With a new occupant in the director's office behind the gift shop, changes in management methods began to appear. Gradually the Compton philosophy of management was crystallizing. It was a philosophy conditioned both by what she was and what she wasn't. She was a former employee of a company which stressed accountability and cost-effectiveness, an emphasis which made an impression even on its scientists. She wasn't, on the other hand, a historian or an anthropologist or an expert in any of the other, specialized fields which, at this time, often provided museums with their administrative leadership. Her model was private industry, not academe.

There was, she was discovering, a feeling quite prevalent in museums that since they did not have a "product," they were not businesses, and therefore, business methods were not applicable. Take the matter of the new label for the Indian pictograph in the museum's front hall. The pictograph's location, on the wall above the wide marble stairway, had always made it difficult to label properly. Why not, someone suggested, attach the label to the upstairs banister? Fine, said Mrs.

Compton, and asked for an estimate. The resulting estimate was only for material and included no labor cost. But there weren't any labor costs, the surprised staffer insisted, since he was providing the labor, was on the staff and got paid anyway. It was difficult, Mrs. Compton discovered, to make him understand that what she was after was a unit cost, something that would tell her whether he should be building a sign or doing something else with his time.

One of the most dramatic—and quickest—turnarounds by the museum, once Mrs. Golden was no longer on the scene, concerned a possible new fund-raising project for the guild. And, as a matter of fact, the guild's board, for several reasons, also had been dragging its feet about trying this project.

Dessie Partenheimer, who hadn't used her real name, Despina, since first grade, was a vivacious southerner-turned-Hoosier, who had moved back to Indianapolis from California in 1961. With her came a husband, two children and two ideas for charity fund-raising projects that would prove to be among the most successful ever staged by Indianapolis women's groups. The first idea went to the first organization which she joined—St. Margaret's Guild, a volunteer organization that raised funds for the county's General Hospital (now Wishard Memorial Hospital). It was for a project that Mrs. Partenheimer had helped start back in Hillsborough, California: a decorators' show house, where interior decorators redid rooms in a large, interesting home, and the public was charged admission to see the results.

In the spring of 1962, Mrs. Partenheimer joined the Children's Museum Guild. For some time, the guild's two big fund raisers had been a September style show and the November dance. Don't you have a fund-raising idea for us? guild members asked Partenheimer. She told them about a project that had been a success back in San Mateo. A volunteer group would take an old house that was about to be torn down, turn it into a spooky, scary witches' lair, then sell tickets to this "haunted house" at Halloween time. That's great, they told her, but don't you have something for Easter? With already-existing September and November commitments, an October project, they pointed out, was not very practical.

So Dessie Partenheimer went to work making dance decorations—and worked and worked and worked. Spectacular decorations that took nearly eleven months to make were, of course, by now a firmly entrenched tradition of guild dances. The theme of the dance was "Treasure Island," and the night of the dance a figure of Long John Silver, which Mrs. Partenheimer and other members had labored hours and hours on, was hardly noticed at all. But a worse blow was to come. Members also had spent hours gluing lace and other frou-frou onto cigar boxes to transform them into little treasure chests. Mrs. Partenheimer timed herself: it took six hours to make one. The night of the dance they were sold for $3 each.

Determined to make her volunteer efforts earn more than fifty cents an hour for the guild, Mrs. Partenheimer dusted off the haunted house idea and again tried to sell it. Guild officers again resisted, primarily because of the timing. Grace Golden also was firmly opposed. It just didn't fit the museum's image, she explained. A small group of guild members stubbornly persisted and finally were able to get the matter brought before the guild membership as a whole for a vote. It passed. At the March 1964 board of trustees' meeting, president Rhodehamel announced that the guild was embarking on a new project called the Haunted House. It was the same meeting at which it was announced that Mildred Compton would be the museum's new acting director.

What hardly anybody knew, however, was that, although Dessie Partenheimer was quite familiar with the San Mateo project in a general way (a good friend had been chairman), she never actually had worked on—or even been in— the California haunted houses. Undaunted, and armed with a letter from her friend in California about how things should be done, project chairman Partenheimer led the sixty-five active guild members into a spring and summer of preparatory activities. Finding a location, of course, was crucial. And here the Indianapolis group significantly changed the pattern of what had been done in California, which would, in the long run, mean more profits from the project. A guild member suggested that the upstairs of the Dreyer building, which the museum, of course, already owned, might be suitable. The beauty of that location was that any physical improvements made to the building (to meet fire codes, handle crowds, etc.) could be retained for another year instead of being lost when the old house was torn down, as was the case in San Mateo.

The road ahead to October was still bumpy, however. Mrs. Partenheimer, never forgetting her fifty-cents-an-hour labors gilding cigar boxes, threatened to quit if tickets were reduced to twenty-five cents. (They weren't; she didn't.) Then there was a museum policy change on serving liquor at the fancy preview party in the museum the night before the opening. As it turned out, the party's celebrity guest of honor, an actress named Blossom Rock who played a role in a currently popular TV monster show, was a Christian Scientist and very happy with a dry party.

After thousands of hours of work by guild members and often their husbands, the Haunted House was ready to open to the public on schedule at 1 p.m., Thursday, October 22. The big unknown, though, was how the public would respond.

The house had been planned with scariness and gore appropriate for preteens and teenagers. As a professional nursery school teacher, Mrs. Partenheimer wanted to make sure that children younger than five were not allowed in. And so she stood at the front door, wearing reassuring civilian clothes instead of a witch's costume, holding toddlers whose mothers needed to take older children through. After about three hours, she and other guild members began to realize the public had indeed responded. The line waiting to get in stretched east along Thirtieth Street, around the corner then north up Meridian and out of sight. That night the Haunted House was kept open an extra hour because of the crowds.

Still there were crises. The size of the first day's crowds, combined with the popularity of a spooky, mock rock-group act in one of the rooms, had caused a real bottleneck. Working from the time the doors were shut at 10 p.m. Thursday night until 4 a.m. the next morning, carpenters (donated by the builder-husband of a guild member) cut through the building's thick brick walls and put in two new doors.

Next came the letters to the editor in the local papers, letters that worried about the impact of all this scariness on impressionable young minds. Laughing (a bit nervously), some of the trustees accused Mrs. Partenheimer of planting the letters herself just to increase the gate—and, in fact, the crowds did seem to swell.

Next, a fire department official appeared and threatened to shut down the operation because, he said, the approval that the guild had obtained ahead of time had come from the wrong person within the department. The only way he would let the operation stay open was to have two department men be on duty. Shortly thereafter, complaints began to come from some of the guild members that one of these men was a pincher. (A chagrined fire department replaced him immediately.)

When it was all over, twenty-six thousand people had visited the Haunted House in a ten-day period, and the guild had a record $18,400 to turn over to the board of trustees at the next annual meeting, more than double the guild profits in the past. The style show produced $2,300; the dance, $2,900; and the Haunted House, $13,200. Said board president Rhodehamel, "We are deeply appreciative and somewhat in awe!"

CHAPTER FIFTEEN
Staying Put

One year after being named director of the Children's Museum, Mildred Compton presented her first paper at an annual meeting of the American Association of Museums. Her subject matter, museum volunteers, was timely, considering the herculean efforts of the museum guild during the previous year. And because of her own experience as a guild member, Mrs. Compton was well aware of the substantial contributions, financial and otherwise, that could be made by motivated, well-organized women's volunteer groups.

The 8,321 volunteer hours contributed by guild members in the 1964 calendar year translated to five full-time staff members, she told her convention audience. (Not to mention the fact—and she didn't—that it might be hard to coax full-time staff members into black-toothed witch makeup.)

Another aspect of Mrs. Compton's management style was becoming apparent—a willingness to use the strengths and recognize the talents of others. While Grace Golden had specialized knowledge in several areas touched by the museum collections (eastern European folk crafts, antiques), Mrs. Compton's area of professional expertise (science) was not yet part of the museum's domain. Yet she had no ego problems with going to others for advice. The museum's board of advisors, though often a large board in the museum's early years, currently had only one member—the chairman, Tom Billings. "The trustees aren't using the advisors, so why shouldn't I?"

she reasoned. With the approval of the trustees, she filled some of the slots with technical experts whose brains she could pick with a quick phone call when necessary: Madge Minton, writer, world traveler, wife of Indiana's leading expert on snakes, and herself an ethno-herpetologist; Hubert Hawkins, president of the Indiana Historical Society; Gertrude De Atley, expert on antiques; Harry Tousley, hunter and collector of trophy specimens; Earl Townsend, collector of native Americana.

To increase her knowledge of the museum field as a whole, Mrs. Compton was becoming increasingly active in professional museum organizations. In the fall of 1964 she was named vice president of the Indiana section of the Midwest Museums Conference and, six months later, Indiana representative to that eight-state regional organization's council as well as council vice president. Next, she was elected to the national council of the American Association of Museums—a bit more easily managed, Mrs. Compton was quick to point out, if you were a candidate from among the twenty-five or thirty children's museums instead of from the thousands of art and history institutions.

In 1965, the board of trustees established a pension plan for all employees for the first time. Under its provisions, full-time staff members who had been with the museum at least ten years would be paid, upon retirement at age 65, 1 percent of their salary. The board had also been studying museum salaries for some time in an attempt to codify them. (Previously, salaries were determined and Christmas bonuses bestowed by personal whim, some had complained.) Annual raises totaling $1,620 were recommended in June 1964 by the board's salary review committee, which also announced that, from now on, bonuses—except for a token amount—would be incorporated into salaries. And if museum staff members couldn't be paid like rock superstars, the board decided that at least their salaries could begin to approach those of a profession somewhat comparable—teaching. The recommended goal in late 1964 was to have salaries equal to 85 percent of those paid by the Indianapolis Public Schools.

On January 11, 1966, seventeen months after retiring, Grace Golden died in her home on Riverview Drive in Indianapolis. She was 66. Unfortunately there had never been time to finish the book projects for which she had contracts. Ever aware of the importance of good "position" in newspaper publicity, she undoubtedly would have been pleased with the next morning's *Indianapolis Star*. Her obituary was on page one. The museum—"her" museum for so many years—handled the funeral and burial arrangements. The board of trustees established a Grace Golden memorial fund to perpetuate her name and aims. By fall, the fund, consisting of memorial donations plus part of the money from a refund annuity, had amassed $11,000. Interest from the fund was to be used for educational grants to young people interested in the museum field. The first award went, the following year, to Indiana University anthropology major Bob Breunig, who had been a high school junior volunteer encouraged in his work at the Children's Museum by Mrs. Golden.

A departure from custom, though not from any written policy, occurred in early 1966 when the nominating committee decided to replace Kathryn Ryan, a long-time board member who was resigning (and who obviously was a woman) with Tom Solley, an architect and professor (who happened to be a man). The board of trustees had, in recent years, maintained a careful male-female balance. This new nomination occurred only after "spirited discussion," nominating committee chairman Ray Sweeney reported to the rest of the trustees at the annual meeting. The board's male-female balance "is not absolutely vital to maintain and must fairly be judged secondary to the individual qualifications of candidates for trustee," said the report of the nominating committee (itself consisting of three men and two women). However, the report hastened to add, the committee "nonetheless urges any future nominating committees . . . to make every effort to restore the balance of male-female participation on the board of trustees."

Ironically, a year later, at the completion of his one-year term, this new male trustee, citing the press of academic duties, asked to be relieved of trustee duties and placed instead on the board of advisors. He, in turn, was replaced by the son of the woman whom he had replaced, a candidate of "wisdom, common sense and humor," said the nominating committee. Presumably, the tricky matter of balance was now partially corrected by genes if not by gender.

Several special exhibits during 1966 were helping push attendance to new heights. By year's end, it would reach 135,000, nearly 18,000 more than 1965 and the largest increase so far within a single year. There were exhibits on Lincoln and space photography and a display of the Hallmark greeting card collection. Most extensive was a two-month Indiana Sesquicentennial exhibit and a related ten-day pioneer arts and crafts fair. With the Haunted House continuing to produce profits at a rate that surprised almost everyone, the trustees voted to use that money as a special exhibit purchase fund. Now, for the first time, the museum would have funds it could count on available for additions to the collections.

The two members of the education department were just about swamped as more and more school classes clamored for tours. The museum decided to stay open on Mondays for school visits. A committee from the Indianapolis Public Schools served as advisors for the pilot science gallery which the museum began installing in 1967 (in the room that had been the solarium), after receiving a grant from the Indianapolis Foundation. In the new gallery, designed by Dr. Erwin C. Kleiderer, a retired research chemist, children would learn the basic principles of light, motion and energy. In her annual director's report, Mrs. Compton, mindful that, in the past, some had not thought the Children's Museum should move into the area of physical science, carefully tied the new gallery to the "original aim of the museum [to be] 'interesting and informational.'"

Twentieth century scientific technology moved into another of the museum's galleries as well, but just for the day. At museums and universities elsewhere, X-ray technology was being used as a nondestructive tool for learning more about mummies. One Friday in November 1967, students and doctors from Winona Hospital's school of radiological technology, wearing their green scrub uniforms, arrived at the museum with portable X-ray equipment. The mummy was carefully brought out from behind the glass case and frontal and lateral views were made of the whole body. When other mummies had been X-rayed, the new details didn't always jibe with coffin inscriptions or other information. Fortunately, here the resulting X-rays agreed with what scholars already had determined. This was the body of a woman, and she had lived in a relatively late period—the arms were positioned across the chest, rather than straight down by the sides which was typical of earlier Egyptian burials. In addition, the X-rays added new details to what little was known about Wenuhotep: she was probably in her late teens, she was probably 5 feet, 8 inches tall and weighed between 125 and 135 pounds. Aside from being slightly knock-kneed, the skeleton was in excellent condition and in excellent state of preservation. On her right wrist, Wenuhotep wore an ornament or bracelet. The X-rays were placed on display for visitors to see.

With more visitors and more exhibit material, could the familiar question of more room be far behind? Yet this time there was a determination not to settle for piecemeal solutions, for tacked-on gallery after new gallery. Long-range planning was a concept that board president Rhodehamel had earlier tried to discuss with Mrs. Golden. But it was a concept so far removed from her style of leadership, and from the era in which she had successfully operated, that she probably never actually understood what he was talking about. "What does he mean?" she had said to Millie Compton in some bewilderment. "I don't have time in the day to do what I must do. I don't have time to make long-range plans."

In Mrs. Compton, however, Rhodehamel found a kindred long-range planner. She had become increasingly aware of the great potential of the museum, of the pity of having to keep so much material in storage. She could also see that museums often reacted to an immediate need rather than looking ahead. Witness even the Children's Museum, with its three additions within ten years. Rhodehamel selected as head of the first long-range planning committee Tom Werbe, second vice president of the board of trustees (and husband of another of Mrs. Carey's granddaughters).

The committee didn't actually do much for the first year or two; the members weren't really sure what was expected of them. But out of congenial dinner meetings at the University Club on North Delaware, there began to evolve a sense of what the museum was going to require down the road. Committee members studied reports forecasting the city's future and analyzed how the museum could best play a role in that future. It became apparent that, if the museum were to fulfill the potential that Mrs. Compton and the long-range planning committee felt it had, it would need more room—and more land. At the March 1967 board meeting, the long-range planning committee recommended that the museum begin to acquire more property in the Thirtieth and Meridian area as it became available. And as a matter of fact, the Paller property on Illinois, diagonally north of the museum, was available for $14,000, the board was told. But there was something much more significant in the works.

Back in the 1920s, when the Parry family still lived in the Parry house at 3010 N. Meridian, the two neighboring families in the large homes to the north were the Rauhs, at 3024, and (a postman's nightmare) the Rauchs, at 3050. The two names were even pronounced the same. When Samuel Rauh died, his home, with its hand-carved panels and stained-glass windows, became the Rauh Memorial Library. The Indianapolis school board, which governed the Indianapolis library system at that time, was given rights to the building so long as it was used as a library. But, according to the will (and shades of *The Music Man's* ". . .he left River City the library building, but he left all the books to her. . .") the Rauh house technically still belonged to Sam Rauh's heirs; it would revert to them if the building were no longer used as a library.

The library had, at one time, been a thriving branch, and its proximity was listed as one of the advantages of the museum's moving into the Parry house twenty years earlier. But businesses and other non-family operations (like the museum) steadily were taking over the old homes along Meridian, Delaware and Pennsylvania that once had held library-book readers. At the same time that library use was declining, the expenses of maintaining an aging house were increasing.

Like River City, Indianapolis had a problem. For the city to pull out the library and "give away" (or so it would undoubtedly appear to the public) the building to Rauh's financially well-heeled heirs would be political dynamite. On the other hand, if the city were somehow able to circumvent the will and hang on to the empty building, it would be in an awkward position if it forced a nonprofit, public-serving organization (the museum) to pay fair market value for the property, yet criticized if it didn't. A dilemma indeed.

Enter now not Robert Preston and seventy-six trombones but John G. Rauh, Jr. Attorney Rauh, past president of the museum's board of trustees and currently first vice president, knew the territory both personally (he grew up in the Rauh house north of the Rauh house) and legally.

"Reversionary rights" is the kind of phrase that makes a lawyer's eyes light up. Not only did Jack Rauh understand its implications, but he discovered that the heirs had never received the "substantial" tax benefits available if rights to the property were signed over to a nonprofit organization—say, for instance, the Children's Museum. This, the heirs had agreed to do, Rauch announced at the March meeting. Not surprisingly, Rhodehamel cautioned board members to "be circumspect in discussing these acquisitions."

The great importance of the Rauh property to the museum was that, without it, the museum was blocked on three sides—by the Rauh Library on the north and by Meridian and Thirtieth Streets on the east and south. And just as owning Park Place makes Boardwalk more valuable, in this North Meridian Street Monopoly game, the Rauh property in turn made the Paller property behind it (eventually purchased for $12,500) more valuable. At last the museum would have access to Illinois Street.

Even more than land was involved, however. The underlying question was whether the museum should stay at Thirtieth and Meridian, for through the winter there had been in the air the whiff of something else very intriguing. Trustees of the John Herron Art Museum, itself planning a move to the property on West Thirty-eighth Street given it by the heirs of J.K. Lilly, had made an incredibly tempting offer. Would the

Children's Museum be interested in moving with them to the Oldfields estate, in effect forming a culture complex? Land would be provided for a building on the east section of the grounds near Road 421, with the Children's Museum sharing in the expense of maintaining the extensive and lovely grounds. "A magnificent offer," board president Rhodehamel called it. And a difficult decision. The trustees visited the Oldfields estate, and pondered, and visited again.

By September 22, 1967, the long-range planning committee (after carefully polling two absent members by telephone) had a unanimous recommendation to pass on to the full board: thank you, but no. For one thing, there was the fear that the Children's Museum would lose its separate identity, that it would become just the little brother of the larger museum. For another, the present location was considered easier for children to get to. And now with the Rauh property and access to Illinois Street assured, elbow room would be available for the growing years ahead.

The momentous decision was made. The Children's Museum would stay at Thirtieth and Meridian, its location since 1946.

CHAPTER SIXTEEN
I Knew I Could

In 1930, a slim book, destined to become a children's classic, was published about a plucky little engine that said "I think I can-I think I can." Who knows whether the tale's author ever heard of the Reuben Wells? But if ever there was a true-life "Little Engine that Could," it was the stubby, powerful, wood-burning locomotive which labored up and down the steep grade at Madison, Indiana, for thirty years in the late 1800s.

An incline of 2 percent, or 106 feet per mile, is considered steep for railroads. The grade on the Madison hill was 5.89 percent, a 311-foot-per-mile incline, the steepest, standard-gauge main-track grade in the United States. It was astounding to railroaders that a locomotive powerful enough to shepherd cars up and down this hill without using cogs could be designed and built.

In 1869, a year after the Reuben Wells went into service, the British technical magazine *Engineering,* in a lengthy, detailed article, explained to its readers that, though "its size alone is well worthy of attention," it was the "constructive details of the engine which will cause it to be regarded with special interest by locomotive engineers. . . ."

There was more spark and cinder to the description, in later years, from an engineer who had once driven the Reuben Wells. "Quick as a cat," he called the locomotive. When the Reuben Wells was ready to start uphill, he said, the fireman always had beech logs packed into the firebox as tight as cigars in a cigar box.

And who was Reuben Wells? He was the locomotive's designer, a railroad man who came to Indiana in 1852, became locomotive master for the Jeffersonville and Indianapolis line and later served on the board of trustees of Purdue University. (One of Wells' other remarkable achievements during his railroad career occurred later when he was with the Louisville and Nashville Railroad. He planned and directed the changing of the gauge on 1,762 miles of track in eleven different railway divisions, plus rolling stock—all within twenty-four hours.)

The famous locomotive that bore his name was resting quietly in a Pennsylvania Railroad roundhouse in Northumberland, Pennsylvania, when train buff Tom Billings first got a look at it in 1966. Billings, still chairman of the Children's Museum's advisory board, had first heard about the engine a few years earlier from David Peat, an Indianapolis amateur railroad historian. From the Pennsylvania Railroad, Billings had learned that the Reuben Wells, along with other old engines and cars, was in storage in Pennsylvania. So when Billings and his wife decided to take a trip to Washington and Williamsburg, a detour through the little Pennsylvania mountain town of Northumberland seemed like a good idea.

There were only pigeons to greet the Billingses at the old roundhouse. By holding open the door to let in the sunlight, they could just make out details on some twenty locomotives and cars parked in the shadows. About five engines in from the door, Billings saw what he had been looking for—an old engine with a bulbous-topped smoke stack and ten drive wheels: the Reuben Wells. In addition, Mrs. Billings spotted a small car—the kind laymen called a caboose—upon whose sides was lettered "Madison Hill."

Both pieces of equipment were covered with the dust and grime of retirement. There had been earlier years when the Reuben Wells had been on public display—at Purdue from 1905 to 1940, in Ohio, in Chicago at the 1949 World Transportation Fair and even at the Indiana State Fair. Now the uphill push began to get the famous engine permanently back again in Indiana—specifically into the Children's Museum. But on this particularly steep grade there was, in fact, a cogwheel— Indianapolis banker Otto Frenzel. Frenzel's railroading grand-father, according to family tradition, was the engineer on the first locomotive run from Madison to Indianapolis. The reason Billings got in touch with him, however, was that he was a member of the board of directors of the Pennsylvania Railroad.

Back and forth went letters and phone calls between mu-seum supporters and railroad officials. The railroad, as it turned out, was looking for good homes for its steam loco-motives in "soundly financed museums having adequate facil-ities and staffs to provide proper protection and care of their collections," as a letter to Frenzel from the railroad put it.

There was a big problem, however. The Reuben Wells had already been promised to a transportation museum in St. Louis. Despite this discouraging news, the Indianapolis par-tisans did not stop. St. Louis, they pointed out politely to the railroad, was already getting other pieces of equipment from the Pennsylvania Railroad. There was no historical connection between the Reuben Wells and Missouri, so would that mu-seum really mind if this one engine went to Indianapolis?

With an eye on the interesting phrases "soundly financed museums" and "adequate facilities and staffs" which the rail-road had used in its letter to Frenzel, a high-level effort was begun to assure the Pennsylvania Railroad that the Children's Museum in Indianapolis was indeed all of those things. Mr. and Mrs. Eli Lilly were prevailed upon to write supportive letters. Wrote Lilly, "It seems to me that the museum is well built on a bedrock foundation and its future is as well assured as only too few of our human institutions are." At a monthly board meeting of the Pennsylvania Railroad directors in Miami in spring 1967, Frenzel put in a few more good words on the museum's behalf with railroad president Allen Greenough.

The Indianapolis effort made it to the top of the hill. Just a few weeks later, in May 1967, Frenzel was notified that the famous locomotive would come to the Children's Museum. Pennsylvania Railroad officials, said the letter, were convinced they had placed the Reuben Wells "in its rightful setting."

Frenzel passed the letter on to museum board president Rhodehamel, after scrawling across the bottom in pencil, "Now, take good care of it."

The museum was, in fact, busily figuring out how it would do just that. The most economical large building, it was decided, would be a pole barn, the prefabricated aluminum structure often used on farms. The new train shed was to be thirty feet by seventy-two feet and would be located at the rear and slightly northwest of (and attached to) the museum. It would stand behind the Rauh Library on land which would be rented from the school board, still technically administrators of the city's library system. (The library had received permission to continue operating the Rauh branch for a time.)

Pole barn or not, the museum was told it would have to file certified architectural drawings for the building to get a building permit. But it's just a pole barn—no architect designs those, said the museum. Too bad, said Official Bureaucracy. So an architect (embarrassed to be doing such kindergarten stuff) was hired to sketch a standard Farm Bureau Co-op-supplied, prefabricated pole building.

Meanwhile back in Pennsylvania, the Reuben Wells had been shipped from the Northumberland roundhouse to the railroad's repair yard at Altoona. Tom Billings, accompanied by Barney Ziegler, a train buff and museum staff member (repairs and preparation), arrived at Altoona for a breakfast meeting with Pennsylvania Railroad officials. The venerable locomotive was sitting on a flatcar when Billings got his first full-light look at it. But something was wrong. "Where's the bell?" said a worried Billings, aware of the sometimes-uncontrolled acquisitiveness of super-dedicated railroad fan/collectors. Some dusty, heavy wooden boxes, nailed shut, were spotted in the woodbin of the locomotive. When they were pried open, there was the locomotive's proud brass—the whistle, the bell, a sign that said "Reuben Wells"—all safe and ready for polishing, thanks to the prudence of whoever had put the engine in mothballs after its last ceremonial appearance. It was going to take more than polish, however, to get the rest of the engine in shape. The railroad offered to sandblast and repaint it. When the refurbishing was done, an Altoona car shop foreman told the company newspaper, "My men enjoyed this job no end. We only hope the kids have as much fun seeing this bit of history as we did working on it."

By May 1968, the refurbished locomotive was ready to be shipped to the museum, where it would be placed on permanent loan for $1 a year. The railroad, now officially the Penn Central, (the Supreme Court had approved the merger with the New York Central four months earlier) was also making a permanent loan of the Madison Hill car, variously called a tool car, way car, cabin car or caboose. Though of too late a period ever to have worked with the locomotive at Madison, the car had been displayed with the Reuben Wells at the Chicago railroad fair. A special route which would avoid tunnels and other hazards was mapped out for the flatcars carrying the two relics from Altoona to Indianapolis. "Handle carefully in yards and arounds curves. Maximum speed 25 mph," sternly warned the official tan Excessive Dimensions cards that accompanied the pair. When at last the two cars arrived in Indianapolis, museum officials drove down to the railroad yards in Beech Grove on Indianapolis' south side to get a look at the locomotive and tool car waiting patiently in the wings for final arrangements to be completed.

The most convenient rail siding for transferring the locomotive onto a lowboy truck was at the Monon Railroad station, two miles northeast of the museum. But a fifty-five-ton, shed-filling, 100-year-old locomotive could not just quietly be put on display like some small fossil or costumed doll. The occasion obviously called for a brass band, fanfare, waving flags, excitement. A parade was scheduled to take the locomotive ceremonially on the final leg of its journey. Wouldn't it be a nice touch, thought museum planners, to involve Madison, Indiana, the site of the locomotive's triumphs, in the festivities somehow? But the Ohio River town's high school band said it would be unable to participate. (The museum found out later that Madison had planned on asking for the locomotive itself and was unhappy to see it go to Indianapolis.)

So it was the blaring trumpets and booming drum of the Central Indiana Council Boy Scout band that led the parade along Thirty-eighth Street on June 11, 1968, a sunny summer vacation day for Indianapolis school children. Next came the Reuben Wells, backing down Thirty-eighth Street just as, in its working days, it had backed down the hill at Madison, controlling the descent of train cars. (The locomotive was moving backwards this time not as an interesting, historical touch, but because of the logistics of getting it into proper position once it reached the museum.) Its distinctively shaped smokestack was back in place, and the round number "35" on the front was shiny with new paint. The brass of the locomotive's whistle and bell gleamed in the sunlight, and from the general vicinity of the cab and the smokestack came faint puffs of "smoke" from a fog machine rented for the occasion.

Tooting along behind the fifty-five-ton guest of honor was a small, colorful crepe-paper replica of "The Little Engine that Could," constructed for the recent "500" Festival parade, held annually as part of the hoopla surrounding the Indianapolis 500-Mile Race. Riding in one of the float cars pulled by the little engine were relatives of the real Reuben Wells—a grandson, great-grandson and three great-great-grandchildren who had come from Florida for the occasion.

As the parade approached the corner of Thirty-eighth and Meridian Streets, where it would turn south, a highway department crew high above in a mechanical "cherry-picker" raised the heavy metal poles and direction signs spanning the street to give the locomotive adequate clearance. With escorting motorcycles buzzing back and forth, the parade proceeded the eight blocks down Meridian to the Children's Museum and then turned onto Thirtieth Street. Leaving its escort units, both crepe-paper and musical, the truck pulling the Reuben Wells swung into the alley behind the museum and turned onto the newly acquired Illinois Street property. The backwards-facing locomotive now was in proper position to be winched forward eventually into the new train shed.

Once the long truck was parked on the west side of the alley, a backhoe, rumbling loudly, began digging a trench in front of the open end of the train shed. The trench would enable the lowboy to back down to the level of the tracks onto which the locomotive would be maneuvered. Inside the train shed, a small knot of museum officials watched as the truck moved slowly backwards on this final part of the journey.

Suddenly, the observers gasped. An area of ground, perhaps a long-forgotten cistern, sank under the weight of the heavy truck, and the locomotive tipped perilously to the side. Museum director Compton, watching with the others, thought that the engine was surely going to go all the way over. But the heavy chains securing the ten drive wheels held fast. The engine hung there, askew but temporarily stable. The original logistics had called for this to be a one-day operation; obviously no one had foreseen this complication. Contractor (and member of the museum advisory board) Harry Tousley called in more heavy machinery, and on the following day, efforts continued to right the locomotive. At one point, a cable, straining against the weight of the locomotive, snapped, sending a heavy (and potentially lethal) hook flying across Illinois Street. To everyone's great relief, it landed, doing no damage. At last the truck was made level again, and the locomotive finally moved into the shed.

After the locomotive was installed, the caboose, with much less ceremony, was brought down from the Monon Station and pushed onto the rails behind it. Underneath the engine was a carefully reinforced pit from which visitors would be able to see the locomotive's understructure. The pit, an expensive addition to the exhibit, was decided upon only after some debate and considerable urging from train buffs.

The stack of newspaper clippings about the engine and its arrival were mounting, but so were the expenses—even with Penn Central picking up the tab for refurbishing and moving the two pieces to Indianapolis. In March, Richard Ruddell, board of trustees vice president and chairman of the Reuben Wells installation committee, had estimated a final cost of $25,000. Though the locomotive's breathtaking tip required an extra day and extra equipment, advisor Tousley gulped and stayed with his original quotation of $15,000 for moving the engine and car from the railhead into the museum train shed. It was about half the actual cost, he noted on a letter with the final invoice.

Even so, "all accounts, as a result of the Reuben Wells, will be depleted," trustees were told at their mid-June board meeting. Tousley-Bixler heavy machinery couldn't help with this fiscal tippage; it was recommended that the board sell some stock to get things back into balance. This was done several months later.

In the meantime, the museum had recruited Junior Historical Society clubs in Indianapolis high schools to spearhead a drive for public contributions toward the cost of the installation. A booth was opened on Monument Circle with a sign, "Drive a Spike for the Reuben Wells." For $1, a contributor got to drive a spike with his name on it into a model railroad track. For $50, the spike was silvered; for $100, gilded.

The guild had also climbed aboard. Haunted House proceeds were helping pay for the engine shed, and a railroad theme was selected for the group's early June luncheon. The sounds (recorded) of whistles, bells and train cars clattering over rails filled the dining room at Meridian Hills Country Club as tables were served by waiters decked out in striped coveralls, billed railroad caps and red bandanas. In the center of the tables were small engines, filled with red, white and blue denim flowers, puffing cotton-ball smoke.

It was late June, on a hot Sunday afternoon, when the ceremony to present the Reuben Wells formally to the museum took place. Twelve hundred red and white invitations had been mailed, and folding chairs were put up in the engine house, as the pole barn was now called. As part of the program, trustee Ray Sweeney, ever the public relations impresario, had conceived a program of "whistle-stop" speeches (two minutes for senate and congressional candidates, three minutes for the mayor) which got local politicos to the ceremony. Up on the temporary stage were several rows of dignitaries, including Mayor Richard Lugar, Congressman William Bray, senatorial candidate William Ruckelshaus (with, appropriately enough, considering the setting, a young daughter sprawled across his lap) and Penn Central assistant vice president J.S. Fair, Jr., out from Philadelphia for the occasion.

At the ceremony's climax, after the presentation speech, Otto Frenzel, representing the railroad, raised and lowered an antique railroad lantern (the traditional railroad signal of "proceed"), then handed the lantern to Harley Rhodehamel, president of the museum board of trustees. On cue, a cord was pulled in the cab of the locomotive towering over the spectators, and the clang from the bell of the Reuben Wells reverberated throughout the metal shed.

It was pure Sweeney and one reason Penn Central public relations man F. C. Rhodes, Jr., in a later letter, called the whole project "a press agent's dream. . . . Mrs. Compton supplied the organizing effort and coordination, Tom [Billings] the enthusiasm, Barney [Ziegler] the rail-fan expertise and Ray—what a tremendous job he did on publicity."

The *Indianapolis News* had even uncorked some vintage William Herschell for the occasion, which, if not specifically about the Reuben Wells, was at least about Madison and trains:

"I've been as far east as Altoony;
my west mark, I think, is K.C.,
But distance ain't been my ambition—
just leave out globe-trottin' fer me
I'll let you ride 'round in th' Pullmans
an' revel in dinin' car fare—
Th' Down-train to Madison's my train—
I'll do all my travelin' there!"

CHAPTER SEVENTEEN
Drowning in Success

The Children's Museum was drowning in its own success. This graphic assessment, made by director Compton at the February 1972 annual meeting, neatly focused everyone's attention on the major problem facing the museum as it entered the decade of the 1970s: more people wanted to visit than could be accommodated.

During 1971, even though attendance from school groups was up 26 percent (and this in a year when school enrollment was decreasing), more than three hundred school class requests had to be turned down. Attendance was also strong from families that just dropped in and grandmothers who proudly brought in visiting grandchildren—the random visitors, as the museum referred to them. Total attendance for 1971 was 183,816.

But even as these statistics were being publicly discussed at the 1972 annual meeting, much preliminary work was already underway to solve the problem. Two years earlier, Kenneth Hartman, a retired engineer, had been brought in by the long-range planning committee to study the museum's physical needs and develop specific recommendations for expansion. For many months, he talked with members of the staff about their need for more storage room and work space as well as just plain more elbow room for the increasing number of visitors.

Several things appeared to be responsible for bringing more people into the museum. The installation of the Reuben

Wells had been followed, a few years later, by another major train exhibit which also had proved to be extremely popular. These trains, however, were small models, a collection of nearly two thousand engines, cars and accessories, assembled over a period of years by Indianapolis investment banker Noble Biddinger. The small, bright, shiny cars, whizzing around on O- and standard-gauge tracks past tiny villages and through papier-mâché mountain tunnels, was every boy/man's Christmas morning dream come true.

At Christmas time, the Biddinger's handsome Tudor-style brick home at Forty-fourth and Park had always been one that families, driving around town to look at seasonal decorations, passed very slowly. A gigantic Christmas tree, ablaze with lights and trimmed with oversize ornaments, always filled the floor-to-ceiling window at the north end of the house. Another part of the Biddinger family's Christmas tradition was not visible from the street. Down in a special room in the basement was the model train layout which had grown from a Christmas present for young John Biddinger in 1950 to an extensive collection of both modern and antique pieces. At the many Christmas parties the Biddingers gave each year, neighbors and friends, after seeing the decorations, often would head downstairs to watch the model trains run.

One day, on the way home from a Park School board meeting, Jack Rauch suggested to Biddinger that the Children's Museum would be a logical place for the collection should Biddinger ever decide to part with it. After Rauch took him to see the museum, Biddinger was convinced. "I couldn't believe what I saw," he said later. "I knew right away that was where the trains should go."

The toy train gallery was installed in the garage behind the Rauh Library after six months and $17,000 worth of remodeling, including adding a short walkway connecting the new gallery with the Reuben Wells train shed. The new gallery opened in June 1970, and Biddinger, well aware of the occasional steaminess of Indiana summers, donated not only the trains, but an air conditioner for the garage-turned-gallery. The 18-foot by 24-foot layout had 450 feet of track, eight operating lines, and a circus train on a siding. Museum staff members made adjustments on the underside of the layout by means of a low, rolling "creeper," the type used by auto mechanics. Non-members were charged an admission of twenty-five cents. (The new exhibit was mentioned, among other places, in an eight-line item in Bill Wildhack's popular "Don't Quote Me" column in the *Indianapolis News*. It was a nice, if probably unnoticed, historical touch: the first newspaper photo ever published of the Children's Museum showed little Billy Wild-hack and his brother George looking at a porcupine fish and other exhibit materials being assembled in the Propylaeum carriage house back in October 1925.)

The opening of the toy train gallery might have been the museum's "swingin'est," as a report at the next annual meeting called it, but it couldn't match the unexpected commotion connected, more or less, with another museum event in the early '70s. The unlikely event for such drama was a sedate Maypole celebration on the museum's front lawn. Spectators had gathered to watch junior docent volunteers dance around a pole, weaving long pastel ribbons into traditional patterns. The museum staff, calculating (rightly) that there would not be a lot of competition for May Day publicity, were delighted when both newspaper and television reporters showed up. But as it turned out, the museum's gentle rites of spring were no match for the action which suddenly erupted at the gasoline station across the street.

A woman somehow had backed her car over two gas pumps, which sent a small geyser of flaming gasoline into the air. "Get out of here," shouted station employees, meaning they wanted her car moved out of the way so they could fight the fire. The shaken and confused woman instead thought they wanted her to leave the station, so she drove away. Station employees chased her down the street, firemen arrived and, because of the chance of explosions, the Maypole dance spectators were all hustled inside the museum. The TV and newspaper photographers whirled around, extremely pleased to be right on the spot for action shots of the whole hullabaloo.

Other events, if not so dramatic, were also slowly increasing the museum's visibility in the community (and, hence, attendance), but it was still an uphill battle to reach some

*Little Mildred Sartor (right),
and big sister Irene.*

*Mrs. William Keller and Mrs. John
Compton work on elaborate decorations
for a Children's Museum Guild dance.*
Indianapolis Star photo

Guild members Mrs. John Partenheimer, Mrs. William Ross and Mrs. David Givens stand in front of the Dreyer building, location of the first Haunted House fund raising project in 1964.
Indianapolis Star photo

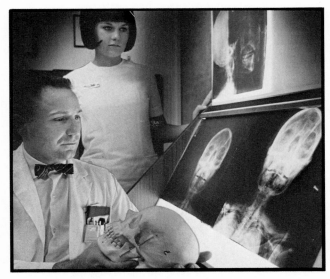

Dr. Saverio Caputi, who directed the examination of the mummy Wenuhotep, compares the resulting X-rays with an anonymous skull. Mrs. John Teike assists.
Indianapolis Star photo

*The Reuben Wells rounds the corner at
Thirtieth and Meridian on the way to its
new home at the Children's Museum.*
Indianapolis Star Magazine photo

*A young visitor scrambles for a look inside
the old log cabin reassembled on the
museum grounds.*
B&L Photographers photo

In the 1960s, the museum's main entrance was at the rear of the addition which included the Hall of Man. At the far right, the newer sections connect with the earlier prehistory gallery and the original Parry house. Kenny Strattman photo

The awesomely large polar bears get much attention from children visiting the museum. B&L Photographers photo

segments of the population, particularly Indianapolis males over 25. This group, of course, included those who controlled corporate purse strings in town. Their standard reaction to the Children's Museum seemed to be, "My wife takes the children, but I've never been." Mrs. Compton had pointedly questioned the museum's image with Indianapolis adults (" . . . why people in this metropolitan city of over a million people love us but don't know us") at the 1970 annual meeting. "Why don't they know," she asked, "that we reach more people in education and cultural pursuits in Indiana than any other institution except for schools? Why don't they know we are a Children's Museum basically because of our superior educational program? Why do they not realize we are the history, anthropology, science and general museum of Indianapolis? Maybe, because we don't tell them?"

Zippy graphic material was one way to spread the word. In 1965, under the direction of trustee Ray Sweeney, a slick, attractive brochure, "A Wonderful Place," had been produced. At the top of its pages were quotations from letters children had written after visits to the museum. "I like the mummy the best," wrote one child. "Will you do me a favor? Keep an eye on that mummy and let me know if anything strange happens."

A few years later, the museum's first annual report, for the year 1969, was published. It was a fairly modest but clever brochure (designed by a local ad agency) with a cover mimicking chalk writing on a blackboard, while statistics and financial reports inside were printed on country-school-homespun, Kraft-type paper. The calendar announcing upcoming activities to members was restyled, and the museum again began publishing a quarterly newsletter. Full-page public service ads about the museum ran in sectional editions of *Time*, *Sports Illustrated* and *U.S. News and World Report*.

In early 1970, the American Association of Museums set up a mechanism for evaluating museums, using certain specific criteria. Those museums meeting the proper standards would be granted official accreditation, much as educational bodies had been accrediting schools, colleges and universities for years. The move to accreditation was partially a response to increased federal activity in the arts, for now government agencies were saying to the museum profession, "Give us some guidelines. What exactly does qualify as a 'museum'?" In June 1970, Mrs. Compton recommended that the Children's Museum apply for accreditation.

As they filled out accreditation application forms and prepared for the site visit, the museum staff discovered there was a lot of truth to one of Mrs. Parkinson's Laws: the only way really to have your home at its best is to have to get ready for company ("For even the most ordinary home needs to be visited just as a book needs to be read"). Some weaknesses "that we had swept under the carpet for many years," as Mrs. Compton was to put it later, now appeared. Written procedures were prepared for all types of emergencies, and specific areas of responsibility were defined for the trustees, director and staff (i.e. "Staff and trustee contact should be encouraged, but personnel problems are decided between the director and staff and administrative decisions between the director and trustees.") Written policies on acquisitions and exhibit philosophy were established.

In October 1971, following a two-day site visit by the directors of the Illinois State Museum and the Children's Museum of Detroit, the Children's Museum of Indianapolis became the first museum in Indianapolis, and one of the first twenty-four museums in the country, to be granted accreditation.

Even with accreditation achieved, there were still areas of the museum's operation to be improved, Mrs. Compton emphasized. As she candidly reported at the next annual meeting, "In preparing for accreditation, we have not succeeded in all our goals, but new, exciting hopes and plans for the future will enable us to correct our deficiencies." And these she ticked off as increasing the ratio of material on exhibit to material in storage; improving the collections records, including using pictures and keeping duplicate records outside the museum; improving the storage conditions; and getting professional conservation help.

Though the museum was aware of its own shortcomings, the four-page report of the visiting committee had been, generally, glowing. "We found the museum presented a far more sophisticated total museum picture . . . than one often finds in children's museums in general across the country." The collections were described as "very extensive, far greater than one would expect to find in a children's museum. Of course, they are uneven in their distribution, but fit [the museum's] needs beautifully, and most of them have been acquired as gifts. The museum has very limited funds for acquisition of collection material." Also, staff salaries, commented the report, "could stand some upgrading."

The museum's location was "ideal" for service to the community, said the report, which also mentioned that the museum was "seriously considering a total major rebuilding as a major institution in the community. Already most of the grounds necessary for this have been acquired and others are readily available." Interestingly enough, the report also mentioned something that was to be as crucial as real estate to the upcoming major building program. In discussing the director's experience ("well-trained") and education ("a Master's degree in a related field of science"), the report added that she was "fortunate to have a background which gave her knowledge and free access to the leading social structure and economic structure of the community."

If the comment had a slightly Nancy Mitford-ish "U" touch to it, it was nonetheless quite perceptive. This "free access" had already been put to work in a way that would be most significant to the museum's building plans and, in fact, its future. Millie Compton had picked up the phone and called George Varnes and said, "George, I need some help."

CHAPTER EIGHTEEN
Bricks, Mortar and Money

It had gone all wrong, somehow. The long-range planning committee was meeting at the home of museum trustee Reily Adams on a snowy, frigid night in late 1970 to hear the latest figures from consultant Kenneth Hartman about what museum expansion would cost in time and money.

The reaction to the figures was as frosty as the night outside. It wasn't the estimated construction time (two years) that was the problem. It was money—a whopping $10 million (which included an estimated $3.5 to $3.7 million in construction money and additional endowment funds to handle the new building's increased operating costs). "The economy's not in good shape. Who knows what is going to happen next year? This is a terrible time to be raising funds," said one of the committee members. The rest of the comments were similarly unenthusiastic.

Millie Compton was furious. After several years of long-range planning and careful analysis of the city's future and the museum's needs (with even preliminary, general discussions of these things with Mr. and Mrs. Eli Lilly), it had all fizzled. The next day, she telephoned one person who had been at the meeting to say how disappointed she had been with the tone of the discussion. "You know, I was too," said the committee member. "I thought everyone was so negative."

"Well, why didn't you speak up?" asked Mrs. Compton.

"I just thought there was something about it I didn't understand," replied the committee member.

A few more phone calls turned up the same reaction—no strong feelings of opposition, after all. It was then that she learned a valuable strategic lesson, Millie Compton was to say in later years: when a new project or proposal is being introduced to a group, make sure the first comments about it are positive, or at least noncommittally neutral. That way, a discussion will at least be started, and if there are any negative comments, they will come out later in conversation. If the first comment is negative, however, those with positive reactions will be reluctant to speak, fearing they have missed something.

How do I get this project back on the track, Mrs. Compton asked board member Fred Hadley, a powerful and blunt-talking Lilly executive whom she had known during her years at the company. Since a board election was coming up soon, why not see if trustee George Varnes could be talked into taking over in 1971 as president of the board, he suggested.

George Varnes had been a friend of John and Millie Compton's from the old Broad-Ripple-neighborhood-Lilly-car-pool days. A native of Kansas, Varnes had come to Indianapolis in 1942 and, in 1954, had been named director of Lilly's fledgling Agricultural and Industrial Products Division, later renamed Elanco. Under his leadership, its growth had been aggressive and strong. In 1969, at Millie Compton's request, he had agreed to serve on the Children's Museum board of trustees. And now, two years later, she had another job for him.

In January 1971, Varnes, group vice president for domestic subsidiaries, was to retire from Lilly at age 61. No more meetings—business or civic—and certainly no more fund raising, Varnes had promised himself. Yet he found himself, a month later, suddenly thrust into a major construction project and building fund drive as the new president of the Children's Museum board of trustees.

Varnes began moving the project forward as if the negative meeting at Reily Adams' (which Varnes, interestingly enough, also had attended) had never happened. It had become apparent that the new facility called for in Hartman's recommendations should be a totally new building, not yet another addition to the Parry house. And though, at first, there was discussion about somehow incorporating the most recent of the museum additions, the 10-year-old Hall of Man, into the new plans, that, too, was soon deemed impractical (one reason was that it did not have footings that could support more than one story).

But before there was much point in determining anything very specific about the form the new structure would take, it was first crucial to see if there were a realistic chance of raising the money needed. For the first time, the museum decided to use the services of an outside, professional fund-raising firm. Varnes, for one, had seen the difference such a firm had made in a building fund drive for his church. Professionals would know exactly how such a fund drive should be organized and would keep after volunteer solicitors until their contacts had all been made—the sort of nagging that was often not only awkward, but usually ineffective for peers to do.

Several fund-raising firms were interviewed. Their proposals were slick, their promises of what they would do for the museum, impressive. But the presentation from one firm was different. Instead of glowing predictions, it reported that the museum had a problem. Ketchum, Inc., with national headquarters in Pittsburgh, already had run several successful fund-raising campaigns in Indiana, which left it not only with a good local record, but with good contacts. A representative of the firm had come to town early to do his own evaluation of the museum and its chances for fund-raising success. Its findings: businessmen had a warm, nostalgic feeling for the Children's Museum and the little sea horse pins from their grade school days. But they knew absolutely nothing about the museum's current operations. Nothing.

Ketchum was hired to do a feasibility study to see what steps the museum should take before a capital fund drive was begun and how much money, realistically, could be raised. The estimate of what actually would be needed also was tightened. In May 1971, the local architectural firm of Wright, Porteous and Lowe, designer of the new Indianapolis Museum of Art building, was chosen (from among five firms presenting proposals) to do an initial survey which would help establish construction costs. The new building would cost about $5 million, said the architects, plus $1 million for exhibits. With the museum's endowment currently at $4 million, an additional $1 million in endowment funds would also have to be raised. (Varnes and the long-range planning committee had adopted the blue-chip expansion dictum—one dollar of endowment for every dollar of bricks and mortar.)

This meant setting a fund-raising goal of $7 million—down a bit from the earlier rough estimate of $10 million, true, but still a lot of money. As Varnes gulped hard, Mrs. Compton was the determined optimist. "We can do it, George, we can do it," she would say. Now it was up to Ketchum to see if that were true.

Dick Davis, a personable young Ketchum representative, arrived in town and opened an office in the Chamber of Commerce Building. Armed with a list of community leaders (not to mention guardians of well-filled pocketbooks, both familial and corporate) who needed to become better-informed about the museum, he recommended a series of "cultivation" parties. These parties, like classy, high-level Tupperware parties, were small gatherings hosted by various museum supporters who would invite the people they knew from the Ketchum list.

Some of these dinner parties, luncheons, and even a breakfast, were at the museum. Others were in the hosts' homes or at clubs. But at all, the program was the same: brief speeches by both Varnes and Mrs. Compton about why a new building was necessary, and then a slide presentation about the museum presented by Davis. As they had been promised ahead of time, guests were not asked for money. However, at the end of the presentation, Davis would say that he would like to see them (the men, generally) at their offices later to get their reactions to what they had learned about the museum.

At the follow-up appointment a week or so later, Davis would ask the party guest's opinion about the museum and its program, whether he thought the $7 million goal could be reached, whether he would be willing to work on a building campaign and whether he or his company would be willing to contribute. After spending the fall on the parties and follow-ups and after interviewing others in the community, Davis and his boss met with Varnes at the museum to report on whether they thought the goal of $7 million could be reached. The verdict was no. In Ketchum's opinion, the museum had set its sights a little high. Varnes listened patiently and then, relishing the drama of it all, pulled from his pocket a letter. "I'd like to show you something," he said.

Back in the spring, when Ketchum had been hired to do the feasibility study, one of the first things the fund-raising firm had done was to hand George Varnes a shopping list of ten specific financial gifts the museum would have to receive if it were to make its goal. It was the kind of shopping that made even the Neiman Marcus catalog look like Montgomery Ward. The first gift was for $3.5 million, the next two gifts were for $1 million, then $500,000 and on down. The ten gifts totaled 85 percent of the $7 million goal.

Accompanied by Millie Compton, George Varnes, list in hand, went down to call at the office of his former boss, Eli Lilly. The elderly gentleman, referred to as "Mr. Eli" by Varnes and others at the company, was fond of Varnes. At Varnes' retirement dinner, Lilly had presented a clever, classical parody-limerick he had written ("An Owed To George Varnes"), in which Varnes was compared to Triptolemos, the Greek who "first taught men about farms . . ." It continued, in part, "As his gifted successor, George Varnes/Weeds crops and fills many barns/He also does fine/Fattening cattle and swine/On good and well managed farms."

In a general way, of course, Mrs. Lilly, the museum's long-time trustee and benefactor, and her husband had been kept apprised of the museum's plans for the future. One evening earlier, in the den of the Lillys' Sunset Lane home, Mrs. Compton and Varnes had been explaining that the necessary expansion meant tearing down the Parry house and its additions. Mrs. Lilly was distressed; she loved the house and the way the museum had grown there. But Mrs. Compton talked convincingly of the museum's crucial space needs if it were to survive and serve Indianapolis children as it should, and why these needs meant a ground-up rebuilding. Varnes talked of concerns about the old building and fire, about the floor load with all those children, about inevitable progress. "Now Ruth," said Lilly gently, "you know what he says is true."

In Lilly's office, Varnes told him that the museum had hired the country's leading fund raiser and showed him the list of major gifts Ketchum said were needed. Lilly Endowment was meeting that afternoon, said Lilly, and he'd just run this by them. "I'm not soliciting this money," said Varnes. "We haven't decided whether we're going to go with this yet, but if we do, this is what they say we have to have."

"Well, let me talk to them," said Lilly. "I'll be in touch."

Shortly before dinner that evening, Varnes got a call at his home. "George," said Lilly, "I talked with the committee about the proposed gift. They're friendly," he said, and hung up. (Incoming Lilly Endowment head Eugene Beesley told Varnes later that Lilly had said to him, "You know, Ruth is very much interested in the Children's Museum." It was, as it turned out, a remark of supreme significance.) Friendly, indeed, they were. Sometime later Varnes received a letter from the endowment announcing a gift of $3.5 million in matching funds. "How do you want it—as an outright grant or as matching funds?" Lilly had asked Varnes. It was the largest single grant the endowment had ever made.

It was this letter that Varnes pulled from his pocket and handed to the Ketchum representatives (who had been told by another Lilly Endowment official that he'd be surprised to see the endowment give as much as $100,000). "You're in," they said. "You've got no problems." But Varnes knew he still had a few. He needed, among other things, two gifts of $1 million.

At the November 1972 board meeting, Varnes announced that, after its preliminary study, Ketchum, Inc. would not hesitate to suggest a campaign objective of $7 million, because of what the firm had determined to be the availability of good leadership, campaign organization personnel, giving potential, image of the institution, acceptability and community mood. (The Lilly Endowment grant was not announced until later in the meeting.) Long-range planning committee chairman Harry Tousley moved that the board commit itself to a capital fund-raising drive. The vote in favor was unanimous. For its services for the coming year of fund raising, Ketchum was to receive $89,500, plus no more than $40,000 for expenses. (Varnes pointed out that this was 1.8 percent of the $7 million.)

The Lilly Endowment grant was to be kept in strictest confidence for five weeks until the public announcement in December. Also in December, trustees were told, they would be asked to have their own personal pledges ready. And, like the good general leading his troops into battle, board president Varnes put on his sword and shield and announced that he and his wife were making a substantial pledge.

With the campaign now official, back Varnes went to Eli Lilly, this time with personal pledge cards. Mrs. Lilly was quite ill, said Lilly, but he would talk it over with her. A few nights later he called Varnes to announce that they were giving $1 million—each. Later in the campaign, when Krannert Charitable Trust had not yet decided how much its grant would be, Mrs. Compton made several calls on Mrs. Herman C. Krannert (her late husband had been chairman of the board of Inland Container). At the end of the campaign, Krannert Charitable Trust, too, made a gift of $1 million.

These other large gifts were not announced right away, for fear others in the community (potential donors as well as workers) would feel their help was no longer needed. Yet no wonder Varnes could say, when volunteers shook their heads with concern about whether the $7 million goal would ever be met, "I'll take book on it. We're going to make it; there's no way we can miss."

But the rest of the money still had to be coaxed from the pockets of Indianapolis; and that might be the hardest job of all. From Fred Hadley had come the idea that it would be good to get a new crop of younger community leaders involved with the museum through the fund drive. Forty-one-year-old Jerome Steketee, an Indiana National Bank vice president, was selected as general chairman. Heading the four campaign divisions were Alexander S. Carroll, master gifts ($25,000 and over); Henry C. Goodrich, primary gifts ($10,000 to $25,000); Robert E. Heine, major gifts ($1,000 to $10,000); and Louis E. Randle, Jr., keystone gifts (under $1,000). This was obviously not going to be a campaign pushing for $5 and $10 donations, though there was an appropriateness to some of those gifts, too (such as the $7.45 from a teacher and first grade students at a Bloomington, Indiana, elementary school).

The names of more than seven hundred workers, men and women, were entered onto the campaign organization sheets. Most of them, of course, were charged with collecting pledges of less than $1,000. The ballroom at Stouffer's Inn, two blocks south of the museum, was jammed at the keystone division's campaign kickoff in mid-June 1973. Through the next weeks, a series of Day-Glo-bright post cards—green, yellow, orange, red—arrived in the mailboxes of workers bearing such messages as "THERE ARE ONLY 3 DAYS LEFT UNTIL JUNE 29!" and "We can't deny any of our prospects the opportunity to participate in this most vital campaign for the progress of Indianapolis. . . . we've extended the deadline . . . until Friday, July 6. WE'VE REACHED 86% !!!"

By the end of July, Ketchum, Inc., its job done, was ready with a report summarizing "outstanding generosity on the part of the Indianapolis community." As Dick Davis put it, "There are some large and significant grants and pledges from foundations and key individuals. But there also is ample evidence that inroads have been made into the commercial and industrial segments of the metropolitan area."

When it was all over, a total of 888 pledges and donations, representing $8,788,897.42, had been obtained. The campaign had shot over the top of its $7 million goal by nearly $2 million.

CHAPTER NINETEEN
Goodbye, Sidney

For anyone who tended to look for such things, the omen from on high was good: this Wednesday morning in September 1973 was sunny. George Varnes took a nineteenth-century wooden shovel (item 73.247.1 from the museum's collections) and, with Millie Compton and Indianapolis Mayor Richard Lugar at his side like prestigious outriders, turned the first symbolic spade of earth for the Children's Museum's new building. Next on the program came the children, two sixth graders from nearby St. Richard's School, introduced as representing "the hundreds of thousands of children of all ages who will benefit from the museum." Using small trowels, they, too, dug into the brown earth at the corner of Meridian and Thirtieth Streets. The ground was officially broken.

One of the great challenges of the whole upcoming construction period was that the museum was to remain open nearly the entire time—trimmed in and modified in what it would offer, of course, but nonetheless open. For the next three years, the museum would operate from a greatly curtailed area, while the brick walls of the new building slowly rose around it. The Hall of Man, the transportation gallery and the train galleries were to be left standing temporarily. Down would come the Parry house (the collections and displays within it had already been moved out) and the Rauh Library building to the north, which had been officially presented to the museum by the Rauh heirs, Mrs. David Chambers, Mrs. Walter Myers, Jr. and John Weldon. After some investigation, interested museum trustees were told that there was, alas, no practical way to save the Parry house's impressive marble staircase, though the stained glass panels from the Rauh house could be preserved (they ended up as decorative panels in the new building's board room and administration area reception room).

With a little more land, a lot of problems would be eliminated, the architects had told the museum board. So in April 1973, (after briefly, in 1971, holding an option on the entire Rauch property), the museum purchased from the Rauch heirs just the vacant lot running from Meridian to Illinois north of the Rauch Library. At that time, the museum tendered to the Rauch family a letter of intent (not binding on either party) to buy the remaining Rauch property if it became available at a "price to be negotiated." (As it turned out, the emotional outcry from some in the city about the Parry and Rauh houses being torn down was one reason, in later years, the museum would back off from buying the Rauch house. Trustees, reluctant to take any more heat about destroying a third Indianapolis domestic landmark, felt, on the other hand, that they couldn't afford to maintain the towering, turreted structure as part of the museum.)

But what was the new museum going to look like? After finishing the preliminary study, Wright, Porteous and Lowe had been picked as the project's architects. (Another small, historic connection: long-time museum trustee Kurt Vonnegut, Sr., had been senior member of the firm when it was Vonnegut, Wright and Porteous, Inc.) Rather than imposing on the structure any predetermined exterior style, the architects and museum representatives decided that the important inside considerations—flow and function—would, in effect, dictate the outside appearance. And the most important consideration from the museum's point of view was how to move great masses of wiggling, laughing, excited children safely and efficiently. The staff was adamantly opposed to escalators for safety reasons, and elevators were not practical with as many as thirty school classes (of some thirty-five children each) sometimes in the building in one day. From Wright, Porteous and Lowe's design department came the idea of wide, gently graded ramps.

Once the idea of the ramps had been accepted, much of the general contours of the building fell into place: there would be a five-story central core with galleries, work areas and offices in wings opening off the core on the north and south. To provide natural light in the building, there would be a peaked skylight at the very top, and the east and west walls of the core would be window walls. (This would eliminate the problem staff members had struggled with for so many years—having to arrange exhibits against wall space broken up by room windows.) These core window walls would be indented, and in this indentation on the west side (Illinois Street), the Hall of Man would remain until the new building was ready for occupancy. When the Hall of Man was finally razed, the area where it had stood would become the main entrance plaza for the new museum.

At last drawings were ready, showing the new building's skeleton with skin on: an exterior of oversized reddish-brown brick and contrasting, inset panels of buff-colored aggregate. It would be a building contemporary in form and feeling. Inside, the "open concept"—exposed pipes and ductwork—and walls of exposed concrete would provide a rough, lean, modern decorative style. Even the holes where metal ties earlier held the wooden forms in place while the concrete hardened would be left visible as a design element.

For some time, representatives from Wright, Porteous and Lowe had been conferring with museum staff members about what would be needed in specific areas—in collections, in the education department, in the exhibits design areas. The collections department was to have a large conservation laboratory, a room where dolls could be mended, exotic shades of paint matched, special glues tested and fragile fabrics cleaned. There was to be limited access to the collections area, a variety of temperature and humidity zones in the large, underground storage rooms and even a cooler for skins and furs. There would be a special fumigation room where almost all new items would make a mandatory stop before going on display or into collections storage.

The exhibits design department wanted galleries with flexible space and ceilings of at least eighteen feet, large rooms for layout and assembly and small, individual two-person studios (with north light) for designers. There would be new silk-screen and paint rooms, carpentry rooms, a model shop, a photography darkroom and a room for a new, large copy camera. The education department wanted a separate entrance for school classes, with its own coat racks, rest rooms and souvenir sales desk; a large, flexible multi-purpose room (with tile floor to handle messy craft projects); and smaller, individual classrooms. There would also be a 350-seat theater, a design challenge since the ceiling was to be an unbroken span and yet also serve as the floor of the administration area above. (Architects designed trusses twelve feet deep and hung the floor between them.)

Staff members fanned out to visit special sites which would give them ideas about both physical facilities and the kinds of displays and exhibits which would eventually go inside this splendid new building. Some places visited were what would be expected—other museums and natural science centers. Other places were a bit more unusual—downtown Indianapolis parking garages to find the ideal slope for the ramps (a wheelchair was taken along on one test trip) and caves in southern Indiana to take pictures and make molds of rimstone dams and stalagmites for use in the natural science area's new simulated limestone cave.

The new building would have 80,000 square feet of gallery space (compared to approximately 40,000 square feet in the entire old building, including work areas and offices). This was being divided into eight major gallery areas, some of which would be ready for the opening and some of which would be phased in during succeeding years.

The ever-popular, but increasingly rickety, plaster cast of the giant ground sloth skeleton was to be replaced by an elaborate display of life-size models of a variety of scary prehistoric animals. (*Tyrannosaurus indianapolitanus*, a consulting Princeton University professor called the largest of the fiber glass replicas when he advised its Chicago creator about such things as the size of the "devil horns" over the eyes and the length of the neck muscles at the back of the skull.)

There was to be a small, walled, outdoor arboretum. A special room was to be designed for Wenuhotep, the mummy. It would be a dimly lighted tomb room, decorated with paintings copied from an actual Egyptian tomb. And on the fifth floor, crowning all of this like the cherry on top of a sundae, was to be a real, operating carousel.

After presentations by several construction firms, the Geupel DeMars company had been chosen by trustees to be construction managers. (It had been a difficult decision for the board, and the vote had been close. Harry Tousley, whose firm also had applied, had energetically served the museum as an advisor and trustee; young Dan DeMars had joined the board in 1970.) The day after Christmas, 1973, mass excavation for the new building had begun, and by the end of January, excavation was 75 percent completed. Geupel DeMars field observation report number seven announced that the bottom of the excavated area, pit run gravel, appeared to be "excellent bearing strata."

Actual construction was started April 10, 1974, and by October, enough of the structure had begun to take shape that museum staff members were given an official walk-through. It was quickly obvious that it was going to take a bit of time for some of them to get used to the aesthetics of the hanging pipes and ducts which were the reality of the architects' "open concept." (As a compromise, in some corridors ceilings were added.)

Others also were shown the building as construction proceeded. Several hard-hat parties for donors and other community leaders were scheduled for late afternoons after 4 p.m., quitting time for the construction workers. This meant there would be enough hard hats available for guests, for nononsense construction-site safety rules precluded any cute, plastic replicas. The reason for these parties was that the museum wanted to keep alive the momentum that had developed during the challenge fund drive. Never again, if it could be helped, would the museum fall back into the amorphous, low-profile position in which Ketchum had found it.

One of the people deeply involved in making sure that the Children's Museum's profile remained high was its public relations director, Polly Jontz. Mrs. Jontz, a past president of the museum guild and one-time *Indianapolis News* editorial staff member, had been doing part-time public relations for the museum since 1963. In 1972, she went to work for the museum full-time. As construction progressed, she and assistant Angie Gordon Woytinek eagerly snapped up all opportunities to get the museum's name and, of course, information about its new building in front of the public.

Banners which said "Children's Museum on the Move" accompanied the two specially designed, 16-ton steel trusses for the theater ceiling when they were transported from Bedford, Indiana, to Indianapolis, and newspapers in towns along the route were sent releases about this important construction material for "the world's largest children's museum." (The new building's total size of 203,000 square feet had nailed down that particular superlative.)

Nothing of any size was just unobtrusively moved from the old building to the new. Firefighting buffs put on old uniforms and drove the three early-era fire engines around the block and then into position on the ground floor of the new building. There was great press and broadcast coverage of the three days it took to ease the Reuben Wells onto its rail siding in the new building (the wall was bricked up behind it). As one television newscaster put it, there were two ways to do anything: the quiet way and the Children's Museum's way.

The topping-out ceremony was obviously just Mrs. Jontz's meat. Much research was done on this originally European construction tradition in which a small evergreen tree (symbolizing good fortune) was fastened to the top beam of a new building. November 14, 1974, was picked for the ceremony, and the construction project manager was asked to have all of his workers line the floors of the building and wave small American flags as a special, gold-painted beam was raised into place. "You want my men to do what?" he asked incredulously. The band from nearby Shortridge High School was to play (though, of course, school had only started two months earlier, and by November, the band still didn't exactly sound as if Sousa were in charge). At last all was ready for the ceremony; the beam had been signed by major donors and other dignitaries, and invitations had been sent out saying, "Look what's under our tree."

Mrs. Jontz hurried back, the night before, from a meeting in Florida to be greeted by snow and the bad news, the next morning, that the crane scheduled to lift the golden beam into position was frozen and would not operate. The only man who could fix it was based in Chicago and his firm couldn't locate him. Then one of the men on the Indianapolis job remembered that the crane expert had an Indianapolis girl friend. Sure enough, he was located right in town and had the frozen machine operating in time for the ceremony. As the beam moved into position, flags waved and the band played patriotic selections (though, considering the crane emergency, "Hooray for Love" would have been just as appropriate).

"In every generation," said construction company executive Dick DeMars in his remarks at the ceremony, "a construction company probably has one job which stands out as the monumental, the most significant, the most important to the community, and there is no doubt in my mind that this will be that job for Geupel DeMars." That evening, new lights twinkled on the midtown skyline as tiny Christmas bulbs on the tree were turned on. The good-luck symbol remained lighted all through the holiday season.

Like a giant cocoon, the new building now surrounded the east end of the Hall of Man; in some places, there was a clearance of only four or five inches between the old and new walls. An inevitable patina of noise and grit from screeching saws and open cement bags now covered life at the corner of Thirtieth and Meridian. And to add to the general confusion, an electrical fire (spotted by a visiting Brownie troop) broke out in the model train gallery one January afternoon in 1974. The working train layout—450 feet of track and seven operating trains—was destroyed. The antiques and other cars weren't however; they were quickly polished and put back on exhibit (in the train shed) within twenty-four hours.

Museum activities continued. In 1974, though 50 percent of the museum's public areas had been lost during construction, 60 percent of the attendance of the preceding year was retained. Staff members and volunteer docents guided visiting school classes through what remained of the old museum building. Other exhibits which had been temporarily dismantled (such as physical science) were taken out to the schools. Mrs. Compton crowded in time for new professional duties as a vice president of the American Association of Museums (as Grace Golden had been before her) and as founding president of the Association of Indiana Museums.

Yet unexpectedly, midst keeping an eye on stacks of change orders, new drawings and innumerable other construction details, the museum's director found herself being squeezed personally and emotionally by the year-long illness and death (from cancer) of her son, John. In September 1973, Steve Sullivan, coincidentally a friend of young John Compton's, had joined the museum as business manager, a post he had previously held at the state library. Now he and other department directors monitored construction progress and kept loose threads from unraveling until Mrs. Compton's attention could return full-time to affairs of the museum.

The grand opening for the new building had been set for the bicentennial year of 1976, on October 2, a date estimated to be as late in the year as possible, yet still offering odds of good weather. At one time, however, it had been hoped that the new building could open in 1975, the year of its fiftieth anniversary. Instead, to celebrate that significant half-century mark, the Newcomen Society in North America (after gentle nudging from the museum's public relations department) picked the museum as the educational institution in Indiana to be honored in 1975. The Newcomen Society, named for English steam engine inventor Thomas Newcomen, was a nonprofit membership organization interested in the history of businesses and organizations in "correlated historical fields." The banquet address, delivered by new museum board of trustees president David Kenny, (and published as a booklet) recounted the history of the museum "through the ambitions, the successes and failures, and the ultimate achievements of those pioneers whose efforts laid the foundations of the particular enterprise," as the general explanatory material about the society put it. Also in honor of the museum's fifty years, a plaque, donated by colorful Indianapolis artist Elmer Taflinger, was placed on the brick wall of the museum's first home, the Propylaeum carriage house, which Taflinger now used as an apartment/ studio.

By June 1975, the ground floor and sub-basement area (with its 22-foot-tall ceilings for storage) had been completed enough for the curatorial staff and collections to move in. Estelle Bell, whose service to the museum reached back to the Carey house and the early 1930s, had completed a monumental inventory (funded by a grant from the National Endowment for the Arts) of the museum's tribal necklaces, sedan chairs, projectile points and peccary bones. Now everything could be moved into the new storage rooms so that the curators and exhibit designers could see exactly what they had to work with as they prepared exhibits for the new galleries.

To warm up the exposed concrete surfaces throughout the building, an orange-paletted color scheme—paints, fabrics and carpets in shades with names like spiced apricot, reef brown, burnt umber and brick—had been chosen by decorator Lee Dorste. In August 1975, the day after rust-colored carpeting was put down, Mrs. Compton and the rest of the museum's administration staff moved into new, third-floor offices.

As always happens, whether it's a simple tract house or a multi-million-dollar museum being built, minor and major design and construction problems surfaced and were sworn at, solved or shruggingly accepted: drinking fountains which showed up sheathed in brown ("Kenya tan"), rather than the requested stainless steel; samples of the outside aggregate panels which weathered into an unacceptable shade and had to be redone many times; a water pipe in a storage area where the museum had emphatically requested there be none. Too late, museum staff members learned that the errant pipe was a trade-off (for a bathroom) they didn't know they had made. (As had been feared, the offending pipe later did spring a leak, spraying irreplaceable material in the collections.) But overall, the imposing new structure was delighting its occupants. At last there was space—and handsome space at that—in which to plan, to store, to design. Preparation of exhibits for new galleries pushed forward on all floors of the building.

In the administration offices, "construction" of a less tangible sort had been going on as well. Under the chairmanship of Polly Jontz, a special committee of business and civic leaders had been established to evaluate and codify the museum's purpose and policies. Part of this process involved studying the museum's image in the community and making recommendations about how the base of community membership and financial support could be broadened. This was no frivolous public-relations, image-fixated concern. Despite (actually, in a way, because of) the splendid success of the challenge fund drive, it was crucial for the museum to have broad support from the community.

Potential tax problems had surfaced shortly after Ruth Lilly's death in March 1973. The Children's Museum, along with several other institutions, was to receive stock from a trust fund which had been established for Mrs. Lilly; this was estimated to be worth a breath-taking $14 million. In addition, lawyers had informed George Varnes, Eli Lilly would be making a bequest to the museum of stock worth about $18 million. The bad news was, however, that these gifts, plus the money given to the challenge fund by the Lillys and Lilly Endowment (and even, perhaps, money from active and retired Lilly employees and their families), might change the museum from a public charity to a private foundation.

At that point, the museum's lawyers were able to convince the Internal Revenue Service that Lilly, the man, was not in control of the museum's operations and had, in fact, never even seen the plans for the new building at the time of the gifts. (The museum qualified as a public charity, it was eventually determined, because a minimum of 10 percent of its income came from public sources, and its directors, activities and members were responsive to the public.) The problem of constantly reminding Indianapolis citizens that the Children's Museum depended upon money from the general public would continue on into the museum's future. And even if there hadn't been the tax legalities, the museum still needed more than just

Lilly money. Construction costs had eased upward from the original $5 million estimate to an eventual total of nearly $6.8 million. ("Because of advanced costs in building construction, funds allocated for exhibits are growing less at an alarming rate," wrote one concerned exhibits advisor in a letter.) Operating costs, of course, would skyrocket once the museum was in its new building.

So, in their quest to broaden community support, the image committee hired a market research firm to check on the Indianapolis public's opinion of and knowledge about the museum. The study's results showed that the respondents knew the museum was for more than just children (87 percent), felt that it needed public support (93 percent), but had never been asked to join the museum (83 percent). Though 40 percent thought that perhaps the name should be changed so that people would not think it was just for children, the committee analyzed the findings and decided there was good potential for membership growth using the present name. (Eli Lilly, upon hearing the question of a name change even being discussed, called Varnes at his winter home in Arizona in great alarm.)

Next, attention was turned to the question of the museum's specific graphic image. It was time, it was decided, for Sidney the Sea Horse to retire. Sidney, however beloved, stood for the old. (As it happened, two years earlier, the museum's long-standing school membership campaign, where Sidney had been particularly prominent, had been terminated. The Indianapolis Public Schools, anxious to halt the distribution of an underground high school newspaper called *The Corncob Curtain*, were forced, by a federal court decision, to stop solicitations by any nonschool institutions.)

In late winter 1975, after several Indianapolis graphic designers were interviewed, Bob Willis of Design Associates was commissioned to come up with a new symbol, "a complete visual identification system . . . to introduce the new and greatly expanded Children's Museum to the public and give it identity for its future," said Polly Jontz in a letter to him.

Willis clapped on a hard hat and followed Mrs. Compton around on a tour of the building under construction. He was impressed with the museum's savvy, its knowledge of what it was, what its product (actually a service) was, and who its market was. "The museum people were supremely secure in what they were doing," he was to say later. Willis and two assistants produced more than one hundred preliminary, rough, thumbnail sketches, and from these, narrowed the possibilities down to a final four. At this point, he broke one of his own rules and showed all four of the final possibilities to the client's representatives "because they were visually sophisticated." There was no doubt about which one Willis thought was best, however: two bright-eyed children's faces tucked snugly into the initials C M were printed in orange on letterheads, envelopes, business cards, even sketches for truck panels that Willis spread out on the table in front of the museum people. The design was clean and spare, the faces of the boy and girl identical except for the hair lines; even the chin lines had been dropped in the name of simplicity, and simplicity was an important design principle of Willis'.

Mrs. Jontz then showed the suggested logo individually to others on her committee. Though a few had reservations that the symbol perhaps said "children" too loudly for a museum that also wanted to appeal to adults, the general reaction was overwhelmingly positive. The Children's Museum had a new symbol. In the months to come, as a slam-bang public relations campaign unveiled the new children's museum to the community (as well as to the rest of the country), the two smiling, bright-eyed children would become nearly as familiar to Indianapolis as the lady on top of the Soldiers' and Sailors' Monument downtown.

CHAPTER TWENTY
Hatching the Egg

It was certainly no thing of beauty, this 6½-inch-long, reddish oval that the exhibit designer was putting into place in the Children's Museum's new third-floor gallery. It was smooth on one end, dissolving into a mass of cracked, crazed rivulets on the other and ending in an abrupt, rough, slicing-off. But then it was one hundred million years old, this dinosaur egg with the fascinating history, an age at which a few cracks and wrinkles are to be expected.

Carefully inked in white on its side was the identifying number 6633. In a museum case in New York City, on the fourth floor of the American Museum of Natural History, was a nest of a half-dozen eggs bearing the identical identifying number; more clutches of eggs with other numbers were elsewhere in the case. All—those in the American Museum and the one ready to go on display in the Children's Museum's new building in Indianapolis—had been among the most publicized of the finds from the most famous of the American Museum's field explorations, the expeditions into Mongolia in the 1920s. "None of the American Museum expeditions experienced more hazards or produced more spectacular finds than the Central Asiatic Expeditions of the 1920s," said *National Geographic* many years later.

Now, fifty years later, the gallery at the American Museum in which the eggs were located was quiet—just the normal number of visitors whose interest was usually drawn to the large dinosaur skeletons in the middle of the room rather than to the display along the west wall, "The Birth, Life and Death of a Dinosaur," which contained the eggs. Yet back in the 1920s, when the dinosaur eggs were first installed in the American Museum, the halls and gallery were packed with people pushing and eager to see them. Outside the museum there were traffic jams, and inside there were overflow crowds at lectures about the discovery of the rare finds. New York City, and, in truth, much of the rest of the country, had gone dinosaur-egg crazy, fascinated both by the ancient exoticism of the fossilized trophies and the handsome, dashing (and sometimes controversial) explorer/naturalist whose expedition brought them back to civilization, Roy Chapman Andrews.

Andrews, a Wisconsin native who had joined the taxidermy department of the American Museum in 1906 fresh out of college, had first specialized in the study of whales and other mammals. Later, as curator-in-chief of the museum's division of Asiatic explorations and research, he had led two expeditions into Tibet, China, Burma and Mongolia before organizing the Central Asiatic Expeditions. These latter expeditions (five of them between 1922 and 1930) were, according to writer Charles Gallenkamp, "audacious in concept, brilliantly planned and executed, . . . the largest, best-equipped and most costly program of land-based exploration ever launched from the United States up to that time."

Andrews, who in later years (from 1935 to 1942) would become director of the American Museum, was no reclusive, self-effacing scientist. An accomplished speaker, he had been able to convey the project's excitement and potential to such financial backers as J. P. Morgan and John D. Rockefeller, Jr. And after the early years of the expeditions he would return to enthrall audiences with tales of exotic discoveries, Chinese bandits and terrifying Gobi Desert sandstorms. He had a taste for polo, beautiful women and publicity—obviously a newspaper writer's dream.

Yet even Andrews was apparently overwhelmed by the publicity and public enthusiasm produced by the eggs. It was disproportionate, he felt, in comparison to that given to some of the expedition's other, perhaps more important, discoveries. Finally he decided to let the dinosaur egg fascination help raise the money needed to continue the expeditions. The American Museum offered one of the eggs for sale to the highest bidder, with the hope that the resulting publicity would produce other donations from the general public as well. The *Illustrated London News* bid $2,000; the National Geographic Society, $3,000; Yale University, $4,000. The winning bid of $5,000 was made by Austen Colgate, who then presented the egg to Colgate University. ("Eggs at $60,000 a Dozen," a magazine titled its article about the auction.)

The beginning of it all had been a year earlier on the first of the American Museum's expeditions into Mongolia. On September 1, 1922, Andrews, paleontologist Walter Granger and their party were traveling in cars over the unexplored, barren interior of the Gobi Desert, on their way to a rendezvous with their camel supply caravan near the Sair-Usu trail. Searching for water, they had finally camped for the night on the floor of a great basin where Mongol nomads had told them a well was located. Off in the distance were spectacular, red, sandstone outcroppings which almost seemed to catch fire in the late-afternoon sun. The Flaming Cliffs, the party named them.

As it turned out, the area where they camped that night supplied more than just water. Wrote Andrews later in his autobiography, "The badlands were almost paved with white fossil bone and all represented animals unknown to any of us. Granger picked up a few bits of fossil egg shell which he thought were from some long-extinct birds. No one suspected, then, that these were the first dinosaur eggs ever to be discovered by modern man—or to be identified. Neither did we dream that the great basin with its beautiful sculptured ramparts would prove the most important locality in the world from a paleontological standpoint."

The following year, back the expedition went to the Flaming Cliffs for more. The first intact dinosaur eggs were found exposed near a ledge; more were quickly uncovered in the sandstone. In shape, the eggs, wrote Andrews, "were elongated, much like a loaf of French bread, and were totally unlike the eggs of any known birds, turtles or reptiles. Two of them, broken in half, showed the white bones of unhatched baby dinosaurs." The dinosaurs which had laid these eggs, covered them with a fine layer of sand and left them to hatch in the warmth of the sun, were identified as *Protoceratops*. They were small (as dinosaurs go), six- to eight-foot-long horned creatures that lived in Central Asia and could be considered ancestors of the giant horned dinosaurs that lived in North America at the end of the Cretaceous period. Though paleontologists earlier had theorized that dinosaurs laid eggs, as do most reptiles, these finds in Mongolia in 1922-23 were actually the first proof that the theories were correct.

In all, Andrews' various expeditions discovered more than seventy eggs at the Flaming Cliffs of Shabarakh Usu. Political upheaval in the area after 1930 (and which continued after World War II) meant that only Russian, Mongol, Polish and Chinese scientists were allowed into the area. In later years, eggs of various types of dinosaurs would be found in France and at a few other scattered spots around the globe, including the United States. "Yet dinosaur eggs are, generally speaking, exceedingly rare," wrote author and dinosaur expert Edwin H. Colbert, particularly "in view of the abundance of dinosaur bones in some regions." Nevertheless, it was the first ones seen—and recognized—by man, those from deep in the Gobi, which caught the world's fancy.

But the trip out of the Gobi Desert in the custody of the Central Asiatic Expedition was only the first step in the journey that would eventually bring one of the ancient eggs to the children of Indianapolis. Though no Chinese bandits or sandstorms were involved in the second part of the journey, before it was all over, getting the dinosaur egg out of Mongolia began to seem like the easy part.

One day in late 1969 or early 1970, a charming (if somewhat eccentric), dapper, white-haired gentleman named Kiefer Mayer arrived at the Children's Museum and announced that he would like to inspect some clothes which had belonged to his mother, Mrs. Charles Mayer, and had been donated to the museum's textile collection. Members of his family had long been associated with the museum. His cousin, Mrs. Russell Ryan, had been a member of the board of trustees for thirty years and her son, John L. Ryan, was currently a trustee.

Mayer looked with interest at the other things Mrs. Compton showed him on a quick tour of the building. And then he made a suggestion of a new item for the museum, a dinosaur egg which belonged to a California friend, the widow of explorer Roy Chapman Andrews. Why didn't Mrs. Compton write and see if Mrs. Street (Mrs. Andrews had remarried) would be willing to part with the egg, he suggested. When it was time for him to leave, he said he was going by taxi cab. Though Mrs. Compton offered to call a cab for him, he said that wouldn't be necessary and headed for the museum's front door. "But you just don't know," thought Mrs. Compton. "Taxis just don't cruise up and down on Meridian." They stepped out the Parry house's front door and he pulled from his pocket a small whistle and blew several short blasts. Up pulled a taxi cab (which had apparently been waiting out on the street); Mayer climbed in and was gone.

When Mayer returned to his home in Arizona, he sent Mrs. Street's address and more information about the egg, plus a picture which Andrews had once allowed him to take of the rare item. According to Mayer, only two of the dinosaur eggs Andrews found were not at the Museum of Natural History in New York—this one, which Andrews had retained for his own personal collection, and the one at Colgate University. Mrs. Street, he wrote "might be induced to dispose of her egg providing it was going to a museum" and if the museum and "some good Hoosier citizen" were interested in having it.

Mrs. Compton wrote to Mrs. Street, telling her about Mayer's suggestion that "the Children's Museum would be a very appropriate place for this egg, where it could be used in the education of more than 170,000 children who tour the museum annually." Mrs. Street replied that she "treasured very much" the egg. "However," she added, "I would consider parting with it at this time if the proper offer were made. . . ."

There was the problem. What, wondered Mrs. Compton, was the proper offer to make for something like this? Upon the advice of Jim Oliver, the director of the American Museum of Natural History, she wrote back to Mrs. Street in February 1970 and offered $500. "I do appreciate the rarity of the egg, but a value, as with most museum material, is difficult to translate into monetary terms. I can only answer in terms of what limited funds we have available for purchase," she wrote. "Your idea of its value may exceed our offer," she continued, "but I can only hope you will be swayed in your decision by the knowledge of its value in the education of children in this area. . . . And children, even more than adults, are concerned with, 'is it real?' "

A rather stiff reply quickly came back from California. "Only because of Mr. Mayer had I vaguely considered parting with the dinosaur egg at this time. I regret I can not accept your offer. Should I wish to find 'a home' for it at some future date I will let you know."

Nothing more was heard of the dinosaur egg for a couple of years until word reached Mrs. Compton that the egg was, as a matter of fact, in Indianapolis—at the Indianapolis Museum of Art. In late 1972, apparently with Kiefer Mayer again as catalyst, Mrs. Street had donated the egg to the art museum. For tax purposes, the egg was theoretically to be given in three annual "pieces." New York appraiser Jerome M. Eisenberg had put a value of $35,000 on it: "Only one other specimen, to my knowledge, has ever been available for sale," said his appraisal. "[It] was said to have been evaluated at and sold for $30,000 a few years ago."

Since Mrs. Street had told the art museum that the egg was too delicate to be shipped commercially, arrangements had been made for a Lilly company plane to pick up the egg in March 1973 on one of its trips to California. At the Monterey airport, the egg was carefully turned over to a Lilly company pilot. "When unpacking," Mrs. Street cautioned in an accompanying letter, "be sure not to lose any of the original sand from the Flaming Cliffs of the Gobi Desert on which the EGG rests."

Yet Mrs. Street apparently continued to worry about the egg and what was being done with it in Indianapolis. In November 1973, Indianapolis Museum of Art curator Paul Spheeris sent her a reassuring letter. "None of the sand on which it rests was disturbed, and on the whole it seems no different than when I saw it in your home. . . . The 'Egg' is now safely in storage awaiting installation. Needless to say, finding related material to put together a meaningful display is of no small consequence. . . ."

The problem was, of course, that putting together meaningful displays about dinosaur eggs fell somewhat outside the normal scope of a museum of fine art. It should go to the Children's Museum, recommended Spheeris; art museum director Carl Weinhardt, Jr. agreed. (In his letter, Spheeris also indicated to Mrs. Street his continuing interest in one of her art pieces, a "polar bear," possibly the white jade polar bear with ruby eyes, said to have been originally from the Czar of Russia and presented to Andrews by a Mongol ruler.)

On the morning of August 26, 1974, after being told that Mrs. Street actually meant for the egg to go to both museums, Mrs. Compton and curator of collections Weimer Hicks picked up, at the Indianapolis Museum of Art, a black, wooden box containing one dinosaur egg on indefinite loan to the Children's Museum. It was arriving just in time to be included in the plans for exhibits for the new building.

The egg was getting closer to actually going on display, though Mrs. Street, in California, apparently did not know this. In October 1974, she wrote to Weinhardt and the art museum, "It is with mixed feelings that I am now turning over to your museum the final one-third undivided interest in my Prehistoric Dinosaur Egg, now in your possession. However, I know you are taking good care of the Egg and I look forward to seeing it in your exhibit some day. . . ."

Mrs. Street seemed not at all surprised at the egg's location when Mrs. Compton later sent her pictures of it on display. However, what did "surprise" her, she wrote back in a letter of thanks to Mrs. Compton, was that she "had never had one word about the 'egg'—tho it had all been arranged thru my dear friend Kiefer Mayer and Mr. Eli Lilly, whose plane came to Carmel to pick it up for the Indianapolis Museum of Art first." (Actually, there had been frequent letters to her from the art museum about the egg.) "I am delighted," she continued in her letter to Mrs. Compton, "that many children can see and enjoy it . . . Someday I hope to see it and your wonderful museum."

In early fall 1976, the reddish-brown oval, which had waited for millions of years in the hot Gobi Desert sands, now waited in its own shadow-box wall display case for the crowds of visitors which would soon visit the Children's Museum's spectacular new building. It was something that could truly supply a "yes" answer to the children's question, "Is it real?"

CHAPTER TWENTY-ONE
Grand Opening

The winner was 6 years old and his mother had not even known he was a contestant. An enthusiastic grade school art teacher had entered a stack of his classes' pictures in the contest the Children's Museum was running to select a poster for the new museum. Among his kindergarten students was Brett Schneider, a quiet, sandy-haired little boy who had produced a tempera painting of a vivid green dinosaur of rather vague zoological classification, with a single eye in the center of its forehead and a mean, smeary, big black mouth. Above the dinosaur, in the typical way young children portray sky, was painted a wide ribbon of blue, and over its shoulder shone a fierce orange sun. The effect was colorful, ferocious and charming.

When the phone call came telling his mother that Brett had been selected as the winner and would cut the ribbon (actually a paper chain) at the grand opening of the new facility, she, at first, didn't understand, and then, didn't believe. But it was true, all right, and on Saturday, October 2, 1976, there stood Brett, blunt-ended children's scissors (gilded for the occasion) in hand, ready to open the new museum officially by cutting the paper chain that stretched across the front door. For the past weeks, his bright green dinosaur had been staring out at Indianapolis from billboards, from posters in bakery windows and on school bulletin boards. And a large, green dinosaur in the (felt) flesh (with a high school volunteer inside) had even been cavorting around at opening week ceremonies.

Director Mildred Compton, trustee George Varnes and Mayor Richard Lugar officially break ground for the museum's new building in September 1973.
Indianapolis Star photo

The log cabin's eventual home would be on the fourth floor of the new building.

The Children's Museum (looking west), before construction of the new building: (1) original Parry house, (2) prehistory gallery, (3) Hall of Man, (4) transportation gallery, (5) log cabin, (6) Dreyer building, (7) Reuben Wells train shed, (8) toy train exhibit, (9) Rauh Library. Dotted line outlines property to be covered by new building and parking lot. Indianapolis Star photo

New building site (looking west) in January 1974, with the Parry house, prehistory gallery and Rauh house gone. The museum was to keep functioning in the remaining buildings during construction. Ray Hartill photo

By July 1975, the new building (looking east) surrounded and towered over the remaining section of the old buildings.
Ray Hartill photo

An evergreen tree symbolizing good fortune was raised to the top of the new building during November 1974 topping out ceremonies.
Grady Franklin photo

*The fiber glass replica of a Tyrannosaurus dinosaur,
created especially for the new museum, arrived in
several sections and was assembled in its new gallery
home.*
Ed Lacey, Jr. photo

*On display nearby was an ancient dinosaur egg from the
Gobi Desert.*
Indianapolis Museum of Art photo

This version had not one eye, but two, and stegosaurian-like ridges down its back.

The Saturday grand opening ceremonies were the climax of ten days of special previews orchestrated by the public relations department. It was a total effort so effective that it later won the Silver Anvil award from the Public Relations Society of America as the outstanding 1976 public relations program in its category. It also was picked for use as a case study in the college textbook, *Public Relations Practices.*

First the press, both local and national, got a look at the new facility. Invitations, mailed out in small boxes, were pieces of a puzzle which, when assembled, said "Now we've got it all together!" On the first floor, in the orange-carpeted open core area created by the ramps, a band played and hors d'oeuvres were served. And to make sure that visiting reporters and editors took a look at all five floors, the bar was placed on the freight elevator (specially decorated for the occasion) and moved from floor to floor. In weeks to come, stories about the new museum appeared on radio and television and all over the country in everything from the *New York Times* and *Redbook* to the *Enid* (Oklahoma) *Morning News* and *My Weekly Reader.*

The next night, there was a formal dinner for the museum's staff, and two nights later, a cocktail party for guild members. The most gala of the galas, however, came three nights later. A gracefully scalloped, long white canopy and red carpet were stretched across the entrance plaza (where once the Hall of Man had stood) to greet the evening's guests: some 400 major donors, plus city and state dignitaries and out-of-town officials from other museums. After a champagne dinner in a festively decorated, temporarily unused third-floor gallery, there was an address by Nancy Hanks, chairman of the National Endowment for the Arts. She brought greetings from President Jerry Ford, who called the new building "a showcase to the nation of what can be accomplished through constructive civic co-operation."

The guests then walked down the wide, carpeted ramps to the museum's new theater for a program dedicating it as the Ruth Allison Lilly Theater. Eli Lilly, who normally seemed to eschew having buildings, or wings or, indeed, auditoriums bear the family name, finally had been convinced that this would be a particularly fitting memorial for his wife because of her long fondness for the institution.

Sometime earlier, shortly after the staff had begun moving into the new building but before there was carpeting or even heat, Lilly and his friend (and fellow museum benefactor) Nick Noyes had been taken on a tour of the building by Mrs. Compton. As Steve Sullivan drove them around in a golf cart, borrowed for the occasion, the two, elderly, white-haired gentlemen were incredulous: "Say, Nick, did you ever think we'd see anything like this?" said Lilly.

"Isn't this marvelous, Eli?" said Noyes. As the cart paused, Lilly, ever the courtly gentleman, suddenly insisted that Polly Jontz, who had been walking alongside, take his seat in the four-passenger cart. It was all she could do to convince him that he should continue to ride.

The program for the theater's inaugural performance had been planned many months earlier when trustee Mrs. J. William Julian, chairman of the dedication evening, and Mrs. Compton had gone to call on Lilly. He had reminisced about music—the opera arias his father used to whistle around the house, the time Metropolitan star Robert Merrill and his wife had been fellow guests at the captain's table during an ocean crossing. Perhaps Merrill would sing, suggested Mrs. Julian. "I think Ruth would like that," Lilly replied.

Sing the powerful baritone did, an eclectic program of Handel, "Porgy and Bess" and "Fiddler on the Roof." There had been a few tense moments earlier when Mrs. Merrill, his accompanist, found the "voicing" of the spectacular, borrowed, 7-foot, 4-inch Bosendorfer grand piano not to her liking. "That's a $25,000 piano—and she's unhappy?" wailed one museum staff member.

Wednesday night's festivities might have had the glitter, and Thursday's (a members' preview) the Indianapolis Symphony, but Friday's event, a party for the neighborhood in the museum's parking lot, had Betty Ford. This event was to thank all those in the area who had been so patient during the construction of the new museum. Some five thousand people had been invited (by fliers hand-delivered to homes within a certain radius) for free hamburgers, ice cream and music by the U.S. Navy Steel Band.

WPA projects had been the lure that brought Eleanor Roosevelt to the Children's Museum back in the 1930s. This time, it was "the statement of faith the museum made in its neighborhood by remaining in its location," as Polly Jontz later put it, that convinced those who arranged the first lady's time to shoehorn an appearance at the museum into her campaign schedule of airplane christenings in Washington, public school dedications in Florida and Chinatown festivals in California. And for a political campaigner, especially one whose husband was running for president, a crowd of five thousand (with a strong representation of blacks) was not to be sneezed at either.

Mrs. Ford, the museum's staff discovered, was a public relations dream. She toured the galleries hand-in-hand with youngsters from a nearby school who had been appointed as her special guides. She posed with a special T-shirt that said "Children's Museum Helper" on the front and "First Momma," (her CB "handle") on the back. She climbed up on a black horse on the fifth-floor carousel and rode sidesaddle, waving and smiling. (In a brief mention in her autobiography written several years later, Mrs. Ford claimed she was actually "irritable because my horse didn't go up and down; it just sat there." True, said the museum, but that was the horse the Secret Service picked because of her bad back.)

Before going out to shake hands in the parking lot, Mrs. Ford met briefly in the small reception room at the back of the theater with museum officials and guests, among them Eli Lilly and George Varnes. Varnes got none of her attention until someone told her that he was the man who had headed the spectacularly successful building fund drive. That made a difference. "I'll have to get to know you better," said she, walking arm-in-arm with him as they strolled back out into the lobby and camera strobe lights flashed.

And then, finally, it was Saturday, the official grand opening. Fittingly, the day's ceremonies were part solemn occasion, part circus. From the nearby Marott Hotel (where museum and city dignitaries had gathered for breakfast) a parade of old-fashioned fire engines, clowns, Boy Scouts, Girl Scouts and the Noblesville High School band moved up Meridian and onto the museum grounds. A magician, who was to perform all day in the museum's theater, entertained the crowd with an escape from a strait jacket while dangling from a crane far above ground. Next, three flags (American, Indiana, bicentennial) were raised on the museum's three 30-foot-tall flag poles as the band played, at the appropriate times, "The Star Spangled Banner," "On the Banks of the Wabash Far Away" and "The Battle Hymn of the Republic."

Then Indianapolis school children presented the museum with writings and crafts, representing art, music, drama and poetry, for a copper time capsule to be buried near the entrance and opened in the year of the nation's tricentennial, 2076. And because, during the early days, children from the city's foreign neighborhoods had proudly donated to the museum items from their families' pasts, the Indianapolis Chinese-American Association now presented to the museum for its collections a fragile, intricate, Chinese paper cutting. It would, the association's beaming president assured Mrs. Compton, bring good fortune to the new building.

At last it was time for Brett Schneider (assisted by Mrs. Compton) to cut the paper chain, and then the two walked into the building hand-in-hand. The museum was now open to everyone. During the next few weeks, it seemed as if just about everyone came, too. More than 200,000 visitors came to see the new building in the first six weeks. That was more than had ever visited the old building in one year. They loved it all—the cave, the big, scary dinosaur, the mummy's hushed new quarters, the new toy train layout, the bright, spacious building itself. But most of all, probably, the children loved the carousel.

CHAPTER TWENTY-TWO
Carousel

Construction of the new building was well underway the day Mildred Compton showed up at one of the weekly meetings and dropped her bombshell. Only at first, Geupel DeMars representative Jim Patterson hardly heard the noise because he thought she was kidding. "What about putting an operating carousel in the building?" she asked him at the end of the meeting.

"I'll have to give it some thought," he replied. When she didn't hear anything from him, she called him. "You were serious," he said a bit incredulously. It was possible, he finally determined, but the only place it could go would be on the fifth level. To get enough room, a support girder would have to be removed, and that could be done only on the top floor where there was no load factor of a floor above to consider.

This particular carousel—or at least its soul and the most important part of any carousel, the animals—had first come oom-pah-pahing into Millie Compton's consciousness during the late 1940s and early 1950s when she took her young children to play in Broad Ripple Park, near their home. It was a great favorite of Sara and Johnny Compton's. To them, and to the other children who rode it, what did it matter that the animals were shabby, that pieces were broken off here and there? But their mother noticed. What few repairs had been attempted were tacky, somehow—glitter sprinkled on some of the animals, for instance. Obviously, the carousel was on its last legs. One day, Mrs. Compton asked the girl taking tickets what would happen to it after it couldn't operate any longer. "Why?" asked the girl. "Are you interested?"

"Yes," replied Mrs. Compton, "if they ever take it apart I'd like one of the animals."

"Put your name on the list," said the girl. Mrs. Compton wrote her name under others on a sheet of paper.

Back in 1917 when this carousel had first arrived in the little country village of Broad Ripple on White River north of Indianapolis, the park was named White City. (This was probably not the park's first carousel; an earlier one, in the peripatetic way of carousels, had come to Broad Ripple from Hartford, gone on to Virginia and eventually made its way to Fort Wayne, Indiana.) White City was a thriving amusement park started around the turn of the century and supposedly modeled after New York's Coney Island. Through the years, its attractions included riverboat excursions, various playing fields, a large swimming pool ("the world's finest") and a midway called Joy Lane with a Ferris wheel, roller coaster and Bluebeard's Fun House. At first, the 1917 carousel was located near the swimming pool in a large, enclosed building with many windows. In 1922, White City was sold and its name was changed to Broad Ripple Park. During the coming years, the park changed hands several times, and the new owner in 1938 moved the carousel slightly south to the playground area and into a pavilion with no sides, but with a high, domed roof.

In 1945, the park and carousel (the rest of the amusement rides had been dismantled many years earlier) were sold to the city of Indianapolis. Then in 1956 (four years after the Compton family moved away from the Broad Ripple Park area), the deteriorating roof of the carousel pavilion finally collapsed, destroying the operating mechanism and scenery panels. The tangled metal and once-jaunty wooden animals were hauled away. And even if there had been an inclination to sell any of the horses or goats or giraffes to private collectors, the list with Mrs. Compton's name on it had, undoubtedly, long since disappeared.

One day, while out in the Broad Ripple area, Mrs. Compton passed by the park and saw that the carousel was gone. Whatever happened to it? she wondered. Where is it now? It was not, however, until she went on the museum staff that Mrs. Compton set out to track it down in earnest—not really for the museum, at this point, but just because she was curious about where it was, why she had never been called and whether whatever was left was being preserved. But this happened to be a time of heavy turnover in the park department's top administration. Mrs. Compton would go down to the park department offices and explain her mission to the current director. "We'll look into it," he'd say, and before anything could happen, he would be replaced.

"Do we have it?" the new man would ask. She would explain—again—that somewhere the department had the parts of a carousel. "We'll look into it," he'd say.

Finally, she was told that, as a matter of fact, the department did have five or six animals, but those were the ones used in Christmas decorations on Monument Circle each year. There had to be more than six, Mrs. Compton insisted. More like forty. At last, word came to her that there were more animals stored in a park department building at Lake Sullivan, and a letter went from Mrs. Compton to park director Lee Burton in late November 1965. (By now, it was not Mildred Compton, private citizen and carousel lover, who was concerned, but Mildred Compton, museum director.) "We wonder," she wrote, "if you might not, on our behalf, appeal to your board so that the children of Indianapolis will be able to see these lovely figures. . . ." The Children's Museum, she continued, "would seem to be the perfect place to preserve that part of Indianapolis which holds so many fond memories for so many of us. . . ." Her letter was accompanied by a letter from Alex Clark, former mayor of Indianapolis and husband of former guild president (and soon to be museum trustee) Margaret Clark.

O.K., you can have two animals, replied the park department. This was not at all what Mrs. Compton now had in mind, but it was better than nothing. A week before Christmas, two horses were picked up by a museum truck at a park department building at Lake Sullivan. During the following spring and summer, guild member Mrs. William Keller, who had been persuaded to take on the job of refinishing the horses, removed their old, flaked and faded paint, repainted one and finished the other in lemon oil so that the carving could be more easily studied.

Replacing the tails also turned out to be a challenge. At first, horsehair switches, the kind sold to augment the tails of show horses, had been considered, but they were too expensive. Then someone suggested that Mrs. Compton could get all the tails she needed—at an abattoir. Off the museum director went to a downtown slaughterhouse. It was, if anything, worse than she had anticipated. She could have as many tails as she wanted, said the burly man in charge, his work clothes splattered with blood. "What colors do you have?" she asked, as if she were shopping for a new hat. In answer, he led her to a huge, black pile in another room. The stench was terrible, and as she got closer, she could see that the pile was a mound of horse tails, black from the flies which covered it. Scraping aside the salt used as a preservative, the workman pulled out two dark and two blond hunks of horsehair (it had been decided to double them for more fullness) and wrapped them in newspaper.

Once home with her grisly treasures, Mrs. Compton began the long, unpleasant process of soaking and washing. At night, so the neighbors would not see, the Compton children were sent to dump the odoriferous water into the sewer across the street. After two weeks, the tails were clean and the residue of hide, tanned. In September 1966, the two now-proud horses with lovely, full tails went on display at the museum in the marble front entry hall. Two summers later, the park department agreed to let the museum have a giraffe to use in its booth at the Penrod Society's fall outdoor extravaganza on the grounds of the Indianapolis Museum of Art. (It turned out to be a somewhat hazardous excursion for the animal; in the crush of youngsters clamoring to touch and climb up on it, the giraffe got knocked over and its head broken off.)

Still, Mrs. Compton was concerned about the rest of the animals, for she, at last, had seen them. Some were lying on their sides, others leaned against the wall in an unused, second-floor storage area, surrounded by scraps from park department craft classes. Hooves, ears and even legs had been broken off, and some of the once-graceful, hand-carved heads had split and warped. All it would take, she feared, would be for someone who didn't understand their value to say, "Let's get that area cleaned out"—and the irreplaceable wooden figures would disappear forever into the flames of a bonfire. Even a letter to the mayor brought no response.

In November 1969, at a guild dance at the museum, Mrs. Compton happened to mention the plight of the Broad Ripple Park carousel to Wilson Mothershead, chairman of the board of Indiana National Bank and long-time museum supporter. "I've got somebody I want you to talk to," he said, after hearing her tale. Up they went to the museum's second floor where Mothershead introduced Mrs. Compton to John Benbow, the bank's executive vice president. "Tell him your story," said Mothershead. Puzzled, but pleased to have anyone interested, Mrs. Compton repeated it all again. "Those animals ought to be preserved," she concluded.

As it turned out, Benbow was a new appointee to the park board. "We're going to have a meeting next week. Let me bring it up," he said. Benbow's interest did the trick. In December, he told Mrs. Compton that if the animals were as valuable as she thought, then the Children's Museum should have them. "They are . . . to remain at the museum until they are of no further use or the museum is disbanded, where upon they are to be returned to the Metropolitan Park Department," said a department memo.

Early on the morning that the city truck was to pick up the animals and deliver them to the museum, Millie Compton and Polly Jontz (both wearing jeans) arrived at the Lake Sullivan building. By the dim light which filtered in through the loft's dusty windows, they searched under crumpled boxes and faded pieces of crepe paper to find any broken ears, legs and hooves which, they feared, might get left behind. Later that day, a Noah's ark with park department logo on the side pulled into the parking lot at Thirtieth and Meridian. Nineteen small horses, eight big horses, two giraffes, a lion, a tiger and a goat were lifted out and carefully placed in special racks that had been hastily constructed. Wrote Mrs. Compton to Benbow (with the mellow magnanimity of the winner), "The cooperation by the park department personnel in the search for the remaining carousel figures has been splendid."

But now that the museum had possession of the animals, what exactly did it have? At first it was thought that the animals, obviously old, might be German-made. Photographs were sent to carousel expert Frederick Fried in New York City, who replied that "The figures . . . are as American as the Declaration of Independence and, indeed, were made in the same city where that document was conceived and executed . . . ." Gradually, the history of the carousel began to unfold. The animals, it appeared, were made by the Germantown (Philadelphia), Pennsylvania, company of Gustav A. Dentzel, "America's pioneer carousel builder," as Fried called him, probably before 1900. They apparently later were acquired by another well-known carousel manufacturing company, Mangels-Illions, which mounted the animals on one of its new mechanisms. It was this carousel hybrid that arrived in Broad Ripple in 1917.

At first, Mrs. Compton envisioned the animals in a stationary exhibit, sort of a carousel diorama like the one at the Smithsonian Institution. Technically, on paper, the figures still belonged to the park department. "I believe it is your intention to let us use some of the figures from time to time for our displays," wrote Benbow to Mrs. Compton in early 1970. But on the phone a few days later (as Mrs. Compton noted at the bottom of his letter) Benbow assured her that, in fact, they had been "given" to the museum. (They were officially converted from a loan to a donation after the new building opened.) Her plan in the fall of 1973, as she headed to Massachusetts for the first national meeting of a new group of carousel enthusiasts, was to sell or trade some of the smaller animals to raise money to refinish the bigger animals. (Animals on the inside of a carousel are generally smaller and plainer than the flashier, larger animals on the outer circle.)

The carousel experts she talked to there, however, convinced her that the museum was fortunate to have nearly all the animals from a single carousel and that she definitely should not break up the set. We'll help you find a mechanism, they promised; they knew that working carousels, once so plentiful in this country, were fast becoming folk art treasures to be preserved. Even a decade earlier, Fried, in his book, *A Pictorial History of the Carousel,* had found that, of the thousands once manufactured, fewer than one hundred carousels were still in existence and operating in the United States. In most cases, devastating resort and amusement park fires were responsible for their destruction. (Not everyone at the conference was so altruistic, however. One woman collector, who wanted one of the museum's giraffes, told Mrs. Compton to name her own price.)

But back in Indianapolis, the idea of restoring the carousel into operating order seemed less viable as the museum staff began looking into the cost and effort that would be involved. Mrs. Compton found her resolve waivering after she went to see a working carousel, in beautiful condition, that was for sale in Virginia. It didn't cost much more than the estimated cost of totally refurbishing and remounting the one the museum already had. She went to the founder of a prosperous, medium-sized, Indianapolis manufacturing company and explained to him her need for money to purchase the carousel. She was asking for about $35,000; he said that he would give her $500.

"Oh, crimeny," Millie Compton said to herself. "It will take me how many trips to put this together with donations of $500." With all her energy absorbed by the new building plans anyway, she realized, she just didn't have time for this kind of fund raising. "No thank you," she said, and returned to her office, now determined to press on, somehow, in the rejuvenation of the carousel she already had. (In later years, she was to write the man and thank him for his turn-down. To be forced to use this carousel with its strong, historic, local connections was the best thing that could have happened, she told him.)

Yet the quest for the Broad Ripple Park carousel animals was not quite ended. Subsequent research had shown the museum that the original carousel had three leaping stags or reindeer; these had not been in the Lake Sullivan cache. Calls to the park department turned up nothing. "They disintegrated," said one department representative. The museum decided to go public with the problem. Newspaper columnist David Mannweiler ran an item about the museum's contemplated rebuilding of the carousel and its problem in locating the three reindeer and two more horses which were also missing. The museum settled back to wait for a response of some sort. It came in December 1973—a cryptic phone call late one Sunday afternoon to a young man on duty at the museum who had absolutely no idea what the caller was talking about. The park department still has the reindeer, the mysterious caller said, and they will be used in the Christmas Gift and Hobby Show.

Sure enough, when Santa arrived at the Indiana State Fairgrounds where the annual show was being held, he was accompanied by three wooden reindeer. Despite their current North Pole address, the museum knew that, in an earlier life, they had been the three stags on the Broad Ripple Park carousel. Back down to the park department went Mrs. Compton, this time with iron in her voice. She reminded officials that, according to the agreement of several years earlier, the animals were all to come to the museum; the three stags were eventually delivered.

Slowly, two or three at a time so that the operating budget could absorb the expense, the animals were shipped off to be restored by a husband-and-wife team in Cincinnati. Bill and Caroline Von Stein, who had done much museum restoration work but had never before worked on carousel animals, joined the national Carousel Roundtable organization and even visited horse farms and the zoo for guidance on the coloration of the animals.

In November 1975, nearly a year before the grand opening (and with a $15,000 grant for the exhibit from the National Endowment for the Arts), another Mangels-Illions mechanism and a newly constructed platform (covered with indoor-outdoor carpet) were installed in the southwest corner, fifth level, of the new building. They were joined by an old Wurlitzer band organ obtained in San Francisco with a $7,400 donation from the Clowes Fund and brought to Indiana.

Gradually, the platform began to fill with the animals, gorgeous after their Cincinnati rejuvenation. By the time of the grand opening, nearly half of the animals had been installed and were waiting for wide-eyed boys and girls, who, like the first lady, would fuss over whether they got to ride on a jumper.

CHAPTER TWENTY-THREE
Adventure Skyward

Shortly before 8 a.m., the two-tone, 7-year-old Oldsmobile Cutlass Supreme, a torn Haunted House sticker on its rear bumper, eases into the parking space marked Museum Director. Some thirty yards away, flush in the ground, surrounded by bark chips and low euonymus bushes, is a plaque marking the location of the time capsule buried nearly six years earlier at the opening of the new Children's Museum building. Nearby, like sentries, are the museum's three flagpoles. Their snap-hooks and halyards, which clang noisily during even a modest breeze, hang motionless in the quiet June morning. Only a few patches of wet pavement remain from the previous night's rain; in the sky to the east, just visible over the top of the museum building, a pale sun makes a tentative appearance in the still-cloudy sky.

Museum director Mildred Compton walks up the short entrance plaza carrying a dark blue umbrella and two plastic bags filled with speeches, program notes and reports to be read and filed. She has just returned from Philadelphia and the last conference of the American Association of Museums she'll ever attend as director of the Children's Museum of Indianapolis. In four months she will retire from the post she has held for the past eighteen years. She will turn over this handsome building, its full- and part-time staff of nearly 150 and its thousands of treasures to a successor who will be only the fourth director in the museum's history.

At 65, Millie Compton is calm, elegant and confident. "She's always gracious and . . . she's very tough," says Elaine Gurian, director of the exhibit center of the Boston Children's Museum, who spent a week at the Indianapolis museum preparing for the move Boston, too, made into a new building a few years ago. "It's very clear that this is a thoroughgoing professional who has not lost a single piece of what it means to treat people well and be a gracious human being." But, she adds, "There's no doubt that she's the director, and there's no doubt that she knows what she likes and what she wants."

And one of the things Mildred Compton had a definite opinion about was that she would retire when she reached 65. "I have seen instances when people have stayed too long in positions . . . and become less and less able to decide when is the proper time to go," she had said when her retirement had been publicly announced a year earlier.

On this June morning, after trying all three doors to find the one the night staff has left unlocked, Millie Compton enters the building and takes the elevator up one floor to her office. Yes, she says, she did have some thoughts at the recent Philadelphia conference about the festivities in this building a year ago when the national AAM conference was held in Indianapolis. On that gala evening, the now-quiet atrium of the Children's Museum was filled with museum professionals from all over the country celebrating the seventy-fifth anniversary of the AAM. As AAM president Craig Black cut a large white birthday cake, he offered a toast to the evening's hosts, "the premier children's museum." It was a dramatic moment that those connected with the Indianapolis museum would never forget. At this year's conference, says Mrs. Compton, many people were still talking about the evening. "No party will ever match yours," one woman told her.

She walks into the reception area of the administration offices on the third level and flicks on the lights. Her office opens directly off the large administration work area; the office door stands open as it will during most of the day. The open door, the office's physical layout (her secretary sits off to the side) and office protocol make her easily accessible to staff members. The office is spacious. Its south-facing windows frame one of the city's better midtown views: the tall trees, well-kept grounds and attractive brick building that was once the home of United States Vice President Charles Warren Fairbanks and is now headquarters of Indianapolis Life Insurance Company.

Near the windows are five shelves filled with personal and museum mementos—framed pencil sketches of her predecessors, Arthur Carr and Grace Golden; pictures of her children; a construction hard hat painted with flowers; a china sea horse under a glass bell; plaques listing honors and awards; a small black and white photograph of Mrs. Compton, Eli Lilly and others at Lilly's ninety-first birthday luncheon; an engraved dish commemorating the ground breaking of a new building for nearby Meridian Insurance Company, on whose board she serves. (She is also on the board of directors of Indiana National Bank.)

The couch on the east wall is covered in a rust and blue contemporary, floral print, and the Chippendale-style chairs around the room have seats of smoky blue. On the grasscloth-covered wall behind Mrs. Compton's desk is a nineteenth century Japanese carved open-work panel. It is from the museum's collections, as are the tall French marquetry cabinet and standing Chinese Coromandel screen. The office, like its occupant—and, indeed, like the whole building—has style.

Mrs. Compton puts down the bags of conference material beside her desk, unlocks the center drawer to check her schedule for the morning and lights the first of the pack of low-tar, filter-tip cigarettes she'll smoke while at work today. In the administration area's small kitchen next door, Steve Sullivan, recently named to the new post of deputy director of the museum, lines up mugs on the counter, fills them with coffee, and checks to see who, of the trustees who've arrived for an early meeting about museum space needs, takes what in his coffee. Mrs. Compton takes hers black.

The adjacent board room in which the meeting will be held also gleams with gems from the museum's collections, carefully arranged in tall (locked) glass-fronted cabinets. Among the treasures are a small Maria Martinez black-on-black bowl; a pair of rare Dorothy Doughty porcelain quail; several

Brett Schneider, who designed the winning
grand opening poster, assists Mildred Compton
in cutting a paper chain to open the new
building officially.

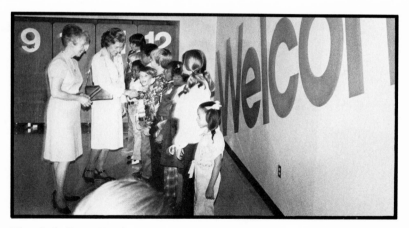

First lady Betty Ford
(second from left)
greets Indianapolis
youngsters during her
visit to the Children's
Museum.
Grady Franklin photo

*The ramps in the building's central core
effectively move visitors from level to level.*
Grady Franklin photo

*Eli Lilly applauds at
the inaugural
performance in the
museum's Ruth Allison
Lilly Theater. Behind
him is the portrait of
his wife which hangs
inside the theater
entrance.*

Wooden animals, hand-carved at the turn of the century, were restored for the carousel on the museum's fifth level.
St. Louis Globe-Democrat photo

Playscape, a special activity center for preschoolers, opened in 1980.
Ed Lacey, Jr. photo

Mildred Compton stands with artist Robert
Indiana's giant numbers, arranged to
commemorate her twenty-one years with the
Children's Museum. She retired as director in
1982. John Brooks photo

The Children's
Museum in 1982, as
seen from Meridian
Street.
McGuire Studio photo

antique (late Edo period) Japanese Imperial Court dolls with hair of shiny black silk floss and robes of colorful brocade; Sheffield silver candlesticks; a scrimshaw pie crimper; and antique toy train cars.

Panels from stained-glass windows, which once gave view of the passing Meridian Street scene from the Rauh house, now hang on the board room wall and in the reception area outside. These days, they are looked at rather than through. Also from the Rauh house is a seven-foot-tall, ornate, Russian grandfather clock which stands in the board room near two large, framed Audubon prints of purple and white herons.

On the north wall hangs the room's only portrait, a Wayman Adams oil painting of Mrs. John N. Carey, given to the museum by one of Mrs. Carey's daughters, Mrs. Morris Haines. The real Mrs. Carey would undoubtedly be amazed at the museum affairs discussed in the board room these days—the budget of $3.2 million and the annual attendance of more than a million which together produce a cost-per-visitor of $2.90 (probably about half the average for the country's museums). Helping support all of this is income from a $33 million endowment; $76,000 from the city of Indianapolis; $20,000 from the Indianapolis Public Schools; nearly $4,000 from township and parochial schools; plus, at least until recent federal cutbacks, funds from the Department of Education's Institute of Museum Services. Earned income (fees from courses, revenue from the gift shop, even $50,000 from twenty-five-cent carousel rides) supplies another $394,000.

In addition, from the private citizens, businesses and organizations of Indianapolis come annual contributions in a variety of categories, ranging from Museum Friends ($25 to $99) to the President's Club (contributions of $1,000 or more, or donations of artifacts valued at least at $5,000 or deferred gifts of $10,000 or more). The President's Club started in 1977 with twenty-five members; in 1981, forty-eight qualified.

There are approximately 5,500 regular museum members—the families with babies in strollers and excited 10-year-olds hurrying up the ramps. This, says the museum, is about the maximum number that currently can be serviced well—at members' nights and in members' classes, for instance. Yet with an average annual attrition of 25 percent (generally people whose children are now grown), more than one thousand new members must be recruited each year to keep the membership figure constant. A goal of the development department, of course, is to convert into donors members whose children are past cave-and-carousel age.

Mrs. Carey would probably be surprised at the size of the board of trustees, as well. It has expanded from the nine men and women who first gathered at her home in June 1925 to twenty-nine active trustees, three ex-officio trustees (representing the Indianapolis school board, the city of Indianapolis and the Children's Museum Guild), twelve honorary trustees and five members of the advisory board. These days, those attending the monthly, late-Tuesday-afternoon board meetings usually overflow the eighteen gold and rust chairs, which surround the twenty-two-foot-long, custom-made, conference table, into the side chairs around the edge of the room.

Today the museum has a staff of seventy-five full-time and approximately seventy part-time employees—a far cry from the early days when Stewart Springer and Arthur Carr labored alone. Yet, as Mrs. Compton points out, "With a staff of more than one hundred, there isn't room for everyone to get to the top. We're always proud of them when they go on to administrative jobs elsewhere." Springer, for instance, the young college student who was the museum's first curator, went on to a distinguished career in marine biology, eventually becoming chief of the Exploratory Fishing Branch of the United States Fish and Wildlife Service and an authority on a group of tiny, luminous, deep-water sharks called Etmopterus lucifer.

Jack McCormick, a Butler botany student who helped with the after-school clubs at the museum in the late 1940s, was, for six years, on the staff of the American Museum of Natural History where he designed the museum's Hall of North American Forests. Carl Armstrong, the museum's bookkeeper in the early 1960s, became director of the Indiana State Museum, and several years later, the Children's Museum's Kathleen McLary also joined the State Museum as curator of education. Bob Breunig, a grade school volunteer, part-time staff member during high school and college and the first recipient of the Grace Golden memorial scholarship, became curator of anthropology at the Museum of Northern Arizona and then chief curator, in charge of the education, exhibits and collections departments, at the Heard Museum in Phoenix.

John Harris, a member of the museum's education department in the late 1960s who wrote the first long history of the museum as his graduate thesis, became director of the Tippecanoe County Historical Museum in Lafayette, Indiana; registrar Deb Richards became registrar at the Dallas Museum of Fine Arts; Dwight Crandell, a recent director of collections, became assistant director of the Museum of Science and Natural History in St. Louis; and public relations and development director Polly Jontz was named director of Conner Prairie Pioneer Settlement in nearby Noblesville, Indiana.

The number of children's museums also has grown from the three (Brooklyn, Boston and Detroit) which the Indianapolis founders knew about when they started their museum in 1925. Yet it's probably no easier to count the number today than it was in 1941 when Eleanor M. Moore wrote in the book *Youth in Museums* that arriving at an accurate figure was "next to impossible . . . they are springing up everywhere almost overnight like mushrooms," she explained, "and frequently . . . close soon after coming into existence." Also, she added, "There are such widely different opinions as to which of those using the name are children's museums and which are not." Even in 1941 there were only eight children's museums housed in buildings by themselves—those in Boston, Brooklyn, Cambridge, Detroit, Duluth, Hartford, Indianapolis and San Francisco. And of the eight, only three, Boston, Hartford and Indianapolis, were entirely independent institutions.

Today, ninety-eight institutions are listed in the AAM's category of children's and junior museums. These include some junior museums which are actually departments of larger, general museums. In addition, there are some museums (science museums, for instance) which don't have "children" in their title, but nevertheless have strong programs for children.

In the eighty-odd years since the world's first children's museum opened its doors, there have been, of course, many changes in the museum profession as a whole. "There's better training, better professional operation, better record-keeping," says Mrs. Compton, who has witnessed much of this change during her years in the profession. Much of this development of professional standards has come as a result of museum accreditation procedures, an area in which Mrs. Compton has been active, having headed the AAM national Accreditation Commission for two terms, from 1976 to 1982. All is more codified: procedures for registering new material, procedures for disposing of no-longer-needed material, even codes of procedures for trustees and staff members who are also collectors.

More than two dozen colleges now offer graduate degrees in museum administration and other specialities within the general field of "museology." With almost-scientific precision, museum visitors are studied and maxims postulated: "The average time you spend at one display is three minutes eleven seconds, and the average number of labels you read is four per exhibit; on walking into an exhibit room of a museum you almost always turn right and you may completely ignore the exhibits on the left-hand side."

Now, six highly successful years after the Children's Museum's move into its new building, several in the museum field have suggested that, if the Children's Museum in Indianapolis has any problems, it is that it really has no problems— that, with the completion of the new building, the top of the mountain has been reached. No problems? At the Children's Museum they would probably smile at hearing that. Work goes forward on a new series of phased additions and modifications to the building. Each department rushes to finish detailed, five-year, long-range plans which chart upcoming exhibits, educational projects and supportive administrative activities. Some staff members struggle with a continual "dichotomy of preservation and education needs," as a 1980 internal appraisal put it—deciding what will be retained and how it will be used. Others work to improve the records of exhibit material, to straighten out paperwork from earlier eras which sometimes leaves something to be desired by current standards (as is the case at many museums).

No problems? Charlie, the boa constrictor, gets out of his cage somehow, and, alas, at about the same time, Erika the long-haired guinea pig disappears permanently. The jumpers on the carousel, because they are so constantly and enthusiastically ridden, need more protection from the overweight of the world. The rule is changed, therefore, from a weight limit (150 pounds) to an age limit (no one over 12 years). "It's easier to say 'You're too old,' than 'You're too fat,' " explains a staff member.

And overall, the museum grapples with something which, if not exactly a problem, is at least a challenge. For much has changed about children's museums since the years when Indianapolis' founders were assembling arrowheads, mounted fish specimens and foreign costumes for children to look at. But then much has changed about children. They live in a world of Muppets and Pac-Man. They want to do things, push buttons, get physically involved with what they are seeing. Some children's museums in the country, like Boston, have put away most of their collections and become primarily participatory experience centers. Others, like Indianapolis, are aiming for a middle course—galleries in which children learn by doing (Science Spectrum, Playscape, the cave) but also more traditional galleries where children learn by looking and even occasionally, praise be, by reading labels.

The direction a museum takes is often influenced by its larger role in the community. In Indianapolis, because there was, for so many years, no history, natural science or general museum, the Children's Museum filled, and is still filling, those roles. In Boston, on the other hand, museums abound. "I think our role is to be the experimental arm of museums," says Boston's Gurian. "We deal with much less didactic information [than Indianapolis does] . . . . We deal with cultural awareness rather than cultural information."

At the Brooklyn Children's Museum, now also in a new building with its share of child-pleasing gimmicks, a docent emphasizes crisply, "We don't allow this to be used as a playground. This is a place to learn—not a school, but a place to learn."

It is still important that museums give children a sense of history, that they pass along the past, says Lloyd Hezekiah, director of the Brooklyn institution. "The definition of the word 'museum' mandates the building have collections," he says. But, he adds, "We all have different philosophies and different approaches."

"I think we can reach a compromise," says Indianapolis' director of collections, Paul Richard. However, he adds, "We've got to find innovative ways to educate with the collections." The mix, so far, seems to be working, at least according to the criteria in an anecdote recounted in a 1937 history of the Boston Children's Museum. A newly appointed museum trustee asked the head "of one of the largest scientific museums in the country how one could tell whether a museum was doing worthwhile work or not. He immediately replied: 'Do the people visit it and use it?' "

In Indianapolis, indeed they do. The great increase in numbers of people visiting the Indianapolis facility since it has moved into its new building has astounded even the staff. And who is visiting also has proved to be a surprise. Whereas in the old building an estimated 50 percent of those attending were random visitors (not part of organized school groups or structured educational activities), in the new building 80 percent of those who walk in the doors fall into that category. Pupils in school groups and others in theater programs, classes and other structured activities now constitute only 20 percent of the total visitors.

Another surprise has been the high numbers of visitors who come with preschool children—as high as 56 percent, according to one survey the museum recently conducted. Part of the reason, theorizes the museum's education director, David Cassady, is that young parents have been influenced by the teachings of child psychologists such as Jean Piaget that "these are the formative years." Also, points out Cassady, "There's a natural monopoly with the preschool child; he's not involved in 'Y,' Scouts and Little League." There is, obviously, an additional challenge to making a museum visit meaningful to a two-foot-tall visitor who can't read. (In the museum's new miniature rooms exhibit, the recessed cases have been placed at staggered heights so that some can be seen by younger visitors.)

The Children's Museum in 1925, the Children's Museum today. In one way they are worlds apart, that tiny collection gathered on a handful of tables and cases in the dusty carriage house, and the five floors of carefully designed exhibits in the spectacular, sophisticated contemporary building. But the reason for their existence, the spirit of what they were and are trying to do, remains the same, transcending years and changed physical and financial circumstances. And another thing remains the same: the look in the eyes—of children studying a mounted porcupine fish in 1925, of children looking at the inside of a space capsule a half-century later.

As Mildred Compton has pointed out, the question children touring the museum most often ask is, "Is it real?". Though the words were more scholarly than the children's, the thought was similar in remarks made at a recent symposium on the future of the American museum. "Direct contact with the object in a society that's wallowing in secondhand images and slides, reproductions and broadcasts," is one of the things museums uniquely offer, said the Museum of Modern Art's Richard Oldenburg. Museums, he continued, supply "an essential sense of the past and present and a continuing linkage with the future; the capacity not only to give people pleasure but to deepen understanding of ourselves and the world around us."

Several years ago, at the time of the Children's Museum's fortieth anniversary, Mrs. Donald Jameson, president of the board of trustees in the 1930s, was among those who sent greetings. She told of the early days and of the contributions made by the museum's founders and early directors. "The rest of us," she continued, "knew we were part of an adventure that was headed skyward."

For the Children's Museum, the adventure continues.

BIBLIOGRAPHY

Allen, Thomas George. *A Handbook of the Egyptian Collection.* Chicago: University of Chicago Press, 1923.

Andrews, Roy Chapman. "Eggs at $60,000 a Dozen." *Saturday Evening Post* 196 (May 24, 1924): 44-47.

Andrews, Roy Chapman. *Under a Lucky Star.* New York: The Viking Press, 1943.

"Authors." *Natural History:* 89 (April 1980): 8.

Babcock, A. D., "The Open Door Museum." *Indiana History Bulletin* 2 (October 1924): 145-147.

Baikie, James. *A Century of Excavation in the Land of the Pharaohs.* London: Religious Tract Society, 1924.

Baikie, James. *Egyptian Antiquities in the Nile Valley.* New York: MacMillan, 1932.

Carr, Arthur B. "In Retrospect—The Early Archaeologist and His Contribution." *Proceedings of the Indiana Academy of Science for 1946* 56: 22-25.

Ceram, C. W. *Gods, Graves, and Scholars: The Story of Archaeology.* Translated by E. B. Garside and Sophie Wilkins. 2nd ed. New York: Alfred A. Knopf, 1967.

Children's Museum Bulletin, October 1932-Spring 1948. Indianapolis: Children's Museum.

Children's Museum News 12: October 1924. Brooklyn: Brooklyn Children's Museum, 1924.

Colbert, Edwin H. *Dinosaurs, Their Discovery and Their World.* New York: E. P. Dutton and Co., 1961.

Compton, Mildred, "A Training Program for Museum Volunteers," *Curator* 8 (December 1965): 294-298.

Dunn, Caroline. *Indianapolis Propylaeum, 1888-1938.* n.p. [1938]

[Howie, Hillis.] *An Expedition for Older Boys to the American Southwest.* n.p. [1938], [1939].

Fenstermaker, Vesle. "Children's Museum Was Lucky Mildred Compton Volunteered." *Indianapolis* (April, 1979): 7-8.

Gallenkamp, Charles. Introduction to "The Fate of the Rash Platybelodon," by Roy Chapman Andrews. *Natural History* 89 (April 1980): 78.

Geib, George W. *Indianapolis: Hoosiers' Circle City.* Tulsa: Continental Heritage Press, 1981.

Gray, Ralph D. *Alloys and Automobiles: The Life of Elwood Haynes.* Indianapolis: Indianapolis Historical Society, 1979.

Griffin, James B. "A Commentary on an Unusual Research Program in American Anthropology." In booklet published at dedication of the Glenn A. Black Laboratory of Archaeology, Indiana University. Bloomington: Indiana University Publications, 1971.

Golden, Grace. "Financing a Private Children's Museum." *Museum News* 39 (April 1961): 26-29.

Golden, Grace Blaisdell. "Children's Museum of Indianapolis." *Childhood Education.* May 1939, 408-412.

Gunther, John. *Inside U.S.A.* New York: Harper and Row, 1946.

Harris, John M. "A History of the Children's Museum of Indianapolis." Master's thesis, State University of New York College at Oneonta, Cooperstown Graduate Programs, 1969.

Henley, Faye. *A Museum Story.* Indianapolis: Children's Museum, 1940.

Hunt, Mabel Leigh. *Matilda's Buttons.* New York: Lippencott, 1948.

Indianapolis Architecture. Indianapolis: Indiana Architectural Foundation, 1975.

Indianapolis Blue Book. New York: The Blue Books Company, 1925.

Indianapolis Council of Social Agencies. *The Leisure of a People: Report of a Recreation Survey of Indianapolis.* Directed by Eugene T. Lies, conducted under the auspices of the Indianapolis Council of Social Agencies and financed by the Indianapolis Foundation. n.p. 1929.

Kellar, James H. *An Introduction to the Prehistory of Indiana.* Indianapolis: Indiana Historical Society, 1973.

Kenny, David H. *Fifty Years Young: The Children's Museum.* Princeton, New Jersey: The Newcomen Society in North America, 1975.

Kuhns, Richard, ed. *The Fifteenth Prairie Trek Expedition 1926-1940.* Thoreau, New Mexico: Cotton-Wood Gulch Foundation, 1940.

Kunitz, Stanley J., ed. *Twentieth Century Authors.* New York: H.W. Wilson Co., 1942.

"The Locomotive 'Reuben Wells'." *Engineering* 7 (February 12, 1869): 106-107.

Magoffin, R.V.D. and Davis, Emily C. *The Romance of Archaeology.* New York: Henry Holt and Co., 1929.

"Money-Making Museum Kits." *Life* 42 (March 11, 1957): 129-130.

Montet, Pierre. *Eternal Egypt.* New York: New American Library, 1964.

Moore, Eleanor M. *Youth in Museums.* Philadelphia: University of Pennsylvania Press, 1941.

Morison, Samuel Eliot. *The Oxford History of the American People.* New York: Oxford University Press, 1965.

Participatory Learning Environment. Brooklyn: Brooklyn Children's Museum, 1975.

Peat, Wilbur D. *Indiana Houses of the Nineteenth Century.* Indianapolis: Indiana Historical Society, 1962.

Petrie, Flinders. *Seventy Years in Archaeology.* New York: Henry Holt and Co., 1932.

Pohle, Gabrielle V. "The Children's Museum as Collector." *Museum News* 58 (November/December 1979): 32-37.

Sayles, Adelaide. *The Story of the Children's Museum of Boston: from Its Beginnings to November 18, 1936.* Boston: George H. Ellis Co., 1937.

Shumaker, Arthur W. *A History of Indiana Literature.* Indianapolis: Indiana Historical Bureau, 1962.

Writers' Program. Indiana. *Indiana, A Guide to the Hoosier State.* New York: Oxford University Press, 1941.

Yearbook of the Society of Indiana Pioneers. Indianapolis: Society of Indiana Pioneers, 1981.

UNPUBLISHED MATERIAL

Much of this book comes from material in the archives of the Children's Museum: minutes of meetings of the board of trustees from 1925 to the present, monthly and annual reports of curators and directors, monthly and annual financial statements, minutes of special meetings, notes for speeches, brochures and newsletters, material assembled for special projects, publicity scrapbooks from 1925 to the present. Organizational work in the archives and research done by former museum staff member John Harris in preparation for a master's thesis (see above) was particularly helpful. Archival material from the Brooklyn Children's Museum also was used.

As mentioned in the preface, sources for specific passages in this book are listed in a footnoted copy of the manuscript deposited in the Children's Museum archives.

INDEX